UNIX in Plain English

Kevin Reichard and Eric F. Johnson

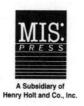

MIS:
PRESS

A Subsidiary of
Henry Holt and Co., Inc.

First printing.

ISBN 1-55828-345-5

Printed in the United States of America
10 9 8 7 6 5 4 3 2 1

MIS:Press books are available at special discounts for bulk purchases for sales, promotions, premiums, fundraising, or educational use. Special editions or book excerpts can also be created to specification.

For details contact: Special Sales Director
                        MIS:Press
                        a subsidiary of Henry Holt and
                              Company, Inc.
                        115 West 18th Street
                        New York, New York 10011

TRADEMARKS:
Throughout this book, trademarked names are used. Rather than put a trademark symbol after every occurrence of a trademarked name, we used the names in an editorial fashion only. Where such designations appear in this book, they have been printed with initial caps.

Project Development Manager: Debra Williams Cauley
Production: Pansy Sapp and Leslie Sharpe

Table of Contents

Introduction

Welcome to *UNIX in Plain English!* This reference work was designed to give you instant access to the UNIX commands and concepts you'll use in your everyday work. In many ways, we merely organized the many handwritten notes sitting next to our terminals and the Post-It notes attached to our monitors in a fashion that benefits both beginning and advanced UNIX users. We too, tired of flipping through disorganized documentation and reference works that were more complex than the documentation.

Why should you need this reference work when you have manuals upon manuals lining your bookshelves, as well as an online help system? To be honest, finding information on UNIX systems is an onerous chore. UNIX documentation tends to lack *any* quick reference: Those manuals provide a wealth of advanced technical information, but they assume a certain level of familiarity with computing in general and the UNIX operating system specifically. Yes, most UNIX systems have online manual (**man**) pages covering the entire command set. But in order to use the manual page, you first need to know the name of the command. Since most of us don't know exactly what we want until we find it—the greatest argument, incidentally, for extensive hypertext help systems—the online manual pages are an ineffective method of learning more about UNIX systems.

UNIX is definitely geared for the educated user. Once you understand the basic mechanisms, commands, and structures, you'll do reasonably well in your everyday work. However, you'll be in trouble if you veer from the basics. That's where *UNIX in Plain English* comes in. For this book, we complied various lists of the UNIX command set: in alphabetical form, by type, and cross-referenced with DOS commands. We also added a section that lists the computer task and then offers the necessary UNIX command, working backward from the usual reference format.

This book was written as a companion to *Teach Yourself UNIX*, second edition (MIS:Press, 1992). We wrote *Teach Yourself UNIX* purely as a beginners' tutorial, although we did include a reference section at the back of that book. *UNIX in Plain English* is meant to be an extension of that reference section. We hope that you'll take the time to look up the extended explanations of important commands in *Teach Yourself UNIX*. While we list most of the command-line options for most UNIX commands in this work, you can find fuller explanations for the major UNIX commands in *Teach Yourself UNIX*. If you're looking for more information about some of the lesser-known UNIX commands, you can either rush out and buy yet *another* UNIX text (we list some essential works in the Bibliography) or check your system documentation.

How This Book Is Organized

We found that our searches for information on UNIX commands were accomplished in several different ways:

- We know exactly what we're looking for, and all we need is the information for a specific command. (As you might expect, this option occurs least often.) In this situation, use Section 4, "UNIX from A to Z," to look for the specific command and where it's listed.

- We're not quite sure what we're looking for, but we know exactly what we want to do. (Again, this option is an unlikely occurrence, since we rarely know exactly what we want to do.) In this instance, use Section 5, "UNIX Commands, Organized by Group," and browse through the subsections—general-purpose, text-processing, communication, printing, and file-manipulation commands.

- We're not quite sure exactly what we want to do, but we have a vague idea. (This occurs more in real life than in computing.) Here, check out Section 2, "UNIX in Plain English," and look for the task that matches your need.

- We're not quite sure exactly what we want to do, but we know it's similar to something that we know how to do. In this situation, use Section 3, "UNIX/DOS Cross Reference," to check out DOS commands and their UNIX counterparts.

- We're totally lost and want to browse through our options. (Bingo!) In that case, dear reader, you'll want to peruse the entire book.

These various situations are why we organized the UNIX commands using lists. Most UNIX reference works present all the UNIX commands in alphabetical order, assuming that you know exactly what you're looking for and, therefore, can look it up in a mondo listing of commands. (Yeah, right.) While we supplied an alphabetical listing of the commands covered in this book (Section 4, "UNIX Commands A to Z"), we also included several other sections that present UNIX commands in slightly different formats. Section 2, "UNIX in Plain

English," presents a whole slew of common computing tasks, along with the corresponding UNIX command. For DOS users, we organized a listing of all DOS commands and their counterparts in UNIX (Section 3, "UNIX/DOS Cross Reference").

The heart of the book—Section 5, "UNIX Commands, Organized by Group"—divides UNIX commands into broad categories (general-purpose, file-manipulation, text-processing, printing, and communication commands). System-administration commands—both for general and privileged users—are covered in Section 6, "System Administration Commands." Section 7, "Shell Commands and Variables," explains the tricky concepts behind the UNIX shell and details how to customize your system to streamline daily chores. Internet travelers will want to check out Section 8, "FTP Commands," for an explanation of this command and a listing of the most useful **ftp** commands. Finally, the Bibliography lists other UNIX texts worth checking out.

Section 5 also tells you where you can find the extended explanation of the command. We organized these explanations into an easy-to-use format: The commands are displayed in large type at the top of the page, followed by sections on usage, examples, options, arguments, related commands, and any other relevant information. We left a lot of space around these command listings so that you can jot down notes for yourself in the margins of a command page.

Conventions Used in This Book

All commands can be found in **boldface** throughout the book. In addition, new concepts are highlighted with the use of **boldface** when first explained. Variables are noted by *italic* type. For instance, when we explain a command where you insert the name of your own filename, we list *filename* in italics. The same goes for *values* that you supply. Commands that are to be typed directly into the system are displayed in a monospaced typeface. In addition, you should be aware of some of the references still used in the UNIX operating system:

- **Bell** Back in the old days of teletype data entry, the machines would feature a bell, much like the typewriters of the era. Because there was often little feedback between a user and the computer, the computer would generate a bell sound to attract the attention of the user, who more than likely was across the room staring out the window. Today, of course, computers don't have bells; they have speakers. A reference to a bell usually means a beep emanating from the speaker.

- **Case** In UNIX, the case matters when you're dealing with files. For instance, **Kevin.report** is different than **kevin.report** and **kevin.Report** and **Kevin.Report**.

- **Keys** Not every UNIX keyboard contains the same set of keys. In fact, keyboards differ quite a bit, as vendors like Sun Microsystems, Hewlett-Packard, DEC, and IBM introduce variations on the standard keyboard. For the purposes of this book, we're not going to get into a discussion of differing keyboards, and for the most part the keys mentioned within this book should be present on all keyboards. However, there are two things you should note: The **Enter** and the **Return** keys are the same (in this book, we'll use **Enter**, since that seems to be the trend in modern UNIX usage), while the backspace key is usually labeled **Backspace**, **BkSp**, or ←.

5

A Word of Warning

Even though this is a comprehensive reference work about the UNIX operating system, we do not include every single option for every single command. In fact, we do not list every single command. To be honest, there are many obscure UNIX commands that you'll never even come close to using. And some UNIX commands have been superseded by newer, more effective commands.

Why not list these commands? Because this book was written with the KISS principle in mind at all times: Keep It Simple, Stupid. We focused on the commands that most beginning and intermediate UNIX users need access to most of the time. Therefore, we do not cover commands like **ar** (archive), since it's highly unlikely that the vast majority of UNIX users will ever need it—and it's also highly unlikely that they'll miss its presence in this book. In addition, we do not cover most of the programming commands in this reference work, though basic commands, like **cc**, are covered.

UNIX Variants

For much of its history, UNIX was developed by a group within AT&T (which AT&T later sold to Novell). Other early UNIX work came from the University of California at Berkeley, leading to BSD UNIX (Berkeley Software Distribution). Most major UNIX vendors took what they thought was the best of the AT&T UNIX, mixed in BSD features, and added their own extensions to the pot, resulting in many close, but still slightly different, versions of UNIX. Currently UNIX is a veritable Tower of Babel, with differing versions from Sun Microsystems (SunOS, Solaris, Interactive UNIX), Hewlett-Packard

(HP-UX), IBM (AIX), SCO (SCO UNIX, Xenix), and Novell (UNIXWare), as well as various Intel-based versions (BSD, Coherent, LINUX).

While vendors are working to eliminate many of these differences, don't be surprised if your system doesn't support all the commands and all the options listed in this book. We've tried to flag the most obvious instances of commands and options that are not found on every system. We tested the commands and options in this book on several systems—an AT&T UNIX PC, Sun SPARC 10, Hewlett-Packard Series 9000/700, Silicon Graphics Indy and Indigo models, and 486 PCs running Interactive UNIX—but in the end nothing in life is guaranteed.

How to Reach the Authors

We welcome your feedback. You can reach us via electronic mail at **kreichard@mcimail.com**. Or if you prefer more mundane means of communication, you can drop us a line in care of the publisher.

1

UNIX Overview:
Commands and Structures

On the surface, UNIX appears to be an unnecessarily complex operating system—just witness the large number of commands listed later in this book. But underneath the surface lies the roots of a very simple and elegant operating system. The details may be complex, but the mechanisms tend toward the simple. A good example is the mechanism for telling the computer exactly what you want to do. If you weren't familiar with UNIX, you might be intimidated by a cryptic symbol on the screen:

$

This is called a **prompt**, and it lets you know that the system is waiting for you to enter a command. Of course, if you didn't have any background or education in UNIX, you would be confused at this point. But once you know that the $ symbol is a prompt and that it indicates that the system is waiting for a command from you, the all-powerful user, then UNIX isn't quite so intimidating as it once was. (Several different symbols are used to denote a prompt, depending on which shell you're using. The Korn and Bourne shells use $ as the prompt; the C shell uses %. But we're getting ahead of ourselves here. At this point, just note the existence of a prompt, and remember that when we use a prompt with an example, you are *not* to type in the prompt symbol when you enter a command line.)

Commands

That sense of enlightenment is furthered when you first learn how to interact with the computer. Remember at all times: *The computer is not smarter than you are.* As a matter of fact, it's a lot dumber. Without instructions—called **commands**—from you, the computer can do little more than sit there and run up the electrical bill. It does exactly as you instruct. The key to getting things done is making sure that what you instruct is what you want done.

With that in mind, you can confidently approach your terminal and enter a command. At the prompt, you enter a command (or multiple commands) as well as any arguments and options; the combination is called a **command line** or **command prompt**. Everything in UNIX is a command, no matter what you're trying to do. To run a program, you actually issue a command. To list the files in a directory, you issue a command. To run a text editor, you run a command.

As you know if you've peeked ahead, UNIX features literally hundreds of commands. Some of the commands are used frequently; for instance, text editors like **vi** or **ed** are very handy for creating short files or memos. Some commands are specific to versions of UNIX, while others can be found in virtually every UNIX variant. This book focuses on the commands that can be found almost everywhere. A typical command line looks something like this:

```
$ ls -l
```

The **-1** (number one, not ell) in this command line is called an **option**. Options and arguments modify the command in some way, usually narrowing the terms of the command. For instance, one of the many options associated with the **ls** command (which lists the contents—or files—of a directory) displays the output in a single column, rather than the default of multiple columns. (As you've probably figured out, this refers to our command-line example in the previous paragraph.) There are *very* few commands that don't have any associated options, and mastering these options go a long way toward simplifying your UNIX usage. (Section 5 "UNIX Commands, Organized by Groups," which summarizes a majority of UNIX commands, stresses options in the Examples sections.)

When you run the above **ls** command line, your terminal will display something akin to the following:

```
$ ls -1
data
financials
personnel
misc
newdata
```

The actual filenames aren't important; for our discussion, the central point is that the files are listed in a single column. Without the **-1** option, the output from the **ls** command would look something like this:

```
$ ls
data    figures    newdata      personnel
misc    expenses   financials
```

This is a very minor example of an option. Most options have more far-reaching results, as you'll find out when you start using options in your daily UNIX usage.

Files

For the most part, commands aren't worth a whole lot if there isn't a **filename** involved. (There are a few exceptions, but those commands tend to be on the limited side, unless your UNIX usage is heavy on finding the current date and time with the **date** command.) Everything in UNIX is a file. And we mean *everything*. A directory is merely a file that represents a grouping of other files. A printer is represented by a file. A device, such as a tape drive, is represented by a file.

On one level, this makes things enormously simple: Commands work (mostly) on files. It's up to you to keep track of what the files represent, which makes things a tad more difficult.

A file is a computer structure used to store information in an electronic format that the computer can use: in bits. A bit is either 0 or 1. When strung together, these bits comprise the characters we all recognize. A file is a method for organizing these bits in a logical format; otherwise, they'd be scattered around a hard disk with no reasonable method of retrieving them.

As mentioned, everything in UNIX is a file. When you run a text editor like **vi**, you're referencing a special file that executes a command. When you edit a file within **vi**, you're working with an ordinary text file. When you print that file with the **lp** command, you're sending it to a file representing a printer. And when you save the file in a subdirectory, you're really storing a reference to the file into a file representing the subdirectory.

Sound confusing? It can be, so don't worry too much about it. As time goes along and you work more with UNIX, you'll see how this all makes sense.

There are four types of files:

- **Ordinary files** can be text files (containing only ASCII characters), data files (for instance, a database file may contain characters other than ASCII characters), command text files

12

(which provide commands to your system), and executable files (programs).

- **Directories** contain information about other files. We cover directories in a little more depth later in this section.

- **Special device files** are the files that control physical aspects of the computer system. For instance, when you use the **tar** command to create a tape archive, you're merely writing files to a file representing the tape drive (usually **/dev/mt0**).

- **Links** allow the same file to be accessed under different names in different locations. Since UNIX is inherently a multiuser operating system, it makes more sense to preserve precious disk-space resources and create links between the same file, instead of allowing each user to have a personal copy of the same file.

Sound confusing? It can be, so don't worry too much about it. As time goes along and you work more with UNIX, you'll see how this all makes sense.

Directories

Where there are files, there must be directories as a method for organizing these files. Without directories, daily UNIX usage—particularly on a large installation with hundreds of users—would be a nightmare as these hundreds of users tried to keep track of thousands and thousands of files, all lumped together.

As you saw in the previous section, a directory is nothing more than a file that references other files. You can think of a directory as a file folder holding files and other directories (which are called **subdirectories**), which in turn can contain more files and additional

13

directories. Every directory is actually a subdirectory of another directory, save one, which is designated by a slash (/). This is called the **root directory**. This is why a filename *always* begins with a slash. A full filename indicates the position of a file within the directory tree. The top of the tree begins with the root directory (/), and that root directory holds other subdirectories (common directories at that level include **users**, **etc**, **usr**, and **tmp**). If you're working on a large system with a friendly system administrator, you've probably been assigned a **home directory**, which is where you begin each UNIX session. This directory is probably contained somewhere as a subdirectory of the **users** subdirectory.

UNIX gives you many commands for creating, deleting, and managing directories. The basics are quite easy: Use **mkdir** to create a directory and **rmdir** to delete a directory (if you have the proper permissions to do so, of course). You'll probably want to create some directories of your own as you go along. The idea is to create directories that match your tasks. For instance, you may want to name a directory **reports** if it contains reports for your boss. When working with directories, however, you'll want to exercise a certain amount of caution, as UNIX assumes that you know what you're doing. For instance, if you use the **rmdir** command to remove a directory, make sure you haven't left anything important within the directory, as UNIX will delete the directory and its contents without as much as a warning to you.

Dealing with directories can be a confusing topic, especially when there are a lot of potential commands involved—a topic that is beyond the scope of this reference work. See the Bibliography for a list of recommended books and tutorials on UNIX usage.

Standard Input/Output

Now that you know about files and commands, we need to explain how to use them.

More than one command can be issued at a time at the prompt. It's not uncommon to see a command prompt begin with a command and an option, followed by an instruction to send the output of that command to yet another command. In UNIXdom, this is called **standard input and output (I/O)** or **redirection**.

We'll illustrate I/O with a common UNIX command, **cat**. Running the **cat** command with no options

```
$ cat
```

allows you to merely enter keystrokes. When you press the **Enter** key, your input will be repeated on the monitor. The keystrokes have not been saved to disk, and once you display them on the screen, they're gone forever. Like most UNIX commands, **cat** assumes that standard input means input from the keyboard, and standard output means display on the terminal. (That's why the use of **cat** with no options or filenames merely displays your keystrokes on the terminal screen.) In this instance, **cat** is of little use, unless you enjoy having the computer mimic your keystrokes.

Cat becomes much more useful when a filename is used on the command line. To display the contents of an existing file onscreen, use the **cat** command along with the filename:

```
$ cat kevin.report
Because of declining sales, I recommend that
we halt production of the 1190-AAA widget
immediately.
```

In this case, we've countered **cat**'s assumption that input will come from keyboard input with a filename. Therefore, **cat** displays the contents of the file to screen, rather than your keystrokes.

With input/output commands, you can direct **cat** to perform many additional functions. For instance, you may want to save your keystrokes to an ASCII file; in this instance, you'd use **cat** as an extremely limited text processor. The following command tells **cat** to send standard input—your keystrokes—to a file named **report.1994**:

```
$ cat > report.1994
```

In this instance, **cat** becomes a very rudimentary text editor. You enter text one line at a time; when you're done entering text, press **Ctrl-D** to end input. (Generally speaking, pressing **Ctrl-D** will end input for the UNIX commands requiring input.)

You can also use **cat** as an alternate method for copying the contents of a file to a new file:

```
$ cat report.1993 > report.1994
```

This command line specifies both input (**report.1993**) and output (**report.1994**). The file **report.1993** remains intact; the contents are copied into the new file **report.1994**. (By the way, this is how UNIX manages printing. A printer is set up as a file. When you print a document, you direct the output of a command to a printer, as referenced by a file.)

Finally, you can append your keystrokes or an existing file to the end of another existing file:

```
$ cat report.1994 >> report.1993
```

Here, you would be copying the contents of **report.1994** to the end of the file **report.1993**. If you wanted to add information directly to the end of the file **report.1993**, use the following:

```
$ cat >> report.1993
```

The above input/output commands are illustrated in Table 1.1.

Table 1.1 Input/output commands

Symbol	Usage	Result
>	*command > filename*	Output of *command* is sent to *filename.*
<	*command < filename*	Input from *filename* is used by *command.*
>>	*command >> filename*	Output of *command* is appended to *filename.*
|	*command1 | command2*	Run *command1*; then send output to *command2.*

Notice that the < symbol listed in Table 1.1 performs the equivalent of the following command, which we covered earlier:

```
$ cat kevin.report
```

You get the same result with:

```
$ cat < kevin.report
```

The difference lies in the manner in which the UNIX shell treats the two commands. In the first instance, the shell treats the filename **kevin.report** as an argument to the **cat** command. In the second instance, the shell treats **kevin.report** as input for the **cat** command.

You can use more than one input/output command in a single command line. For instance, many UNIX commands—especially when working with shell scripts—look something like this:

```
$ command < infile > outfile
```

This tells the *command* to use input from *infile* and send the output to *outfile.*

17

Pipes

Standard input/output can be taken a step further when you introduce another powerful UNIX tool: **pipes**. A pipe is merely a method of sending the output of one command for use as input to a second command. It looks like this:

```
$ command1 | command2
```

This is a **pipeline**. For instance, you may want to sort a file before printing it. In this case, you'd use the **sort** command to sort the file and then send the output to the **lp** command to print the sorted file. (See Section 5, "UNIX Commands, Organized by Groups," for more on the **sort** command.) The resulting command line looks something like this:

```
$ sort textfile | lp
```

You can enter multiple pipes on a command line; our example used one merely for illustrative purposes. Here's an example of a longer pipeline:

```
$ ls *.1994 | grep profits | lp
```

This command line searches for all files ending in **1994** in the current directory, sending the output of that command to **grep**, which searches those files for the string *profits*. **Grep** then sends lines containing that string to the **lp** command, which then prints out the lines.

2

UNIX in Plain English

Most of us know what we want to do when we sit down in front of a terminal. The challenge becomes a matter of figuring out how to tell the operating system exactly what we want to do. Unfortunately, the operating system doesn't make the job any easier; it's not very forgiving if your command doesn't quite match your goal.

This section is for those who know exactly what they want to do and need a lead on the corresponding UNIX command. We've listed common computing tasks in the left-hand column (the *italicized* keywords are in alphabetic order) and the conforming UNIX command in the right-hand column. Most commands are listed a few different ways; for instance, you can find the common **ls** command under both *list* and *file*.

If you want to...	Use the UNIX command...
append other files to an existing file	**cat**
create a tape *archive*	**tar, cpio**
search for *ASCII* strings within binary files	**strings**
search and replace *ASCII* characters	**tr**
create a tape *backup*	**tar, cpio**
print a 10-character *banner*	**banner**
start the *Bourne shell*	**sh**
start the *C shell*	**csh**
perform math *calculations*	**bc, dc**
display current month in *calendar* form	**cal**
call another terminal	**ct**
call another UNIX system	**cu**
cancel jobs scheduled with the **at** command	**atrm**
cancel print job	**cancel**
chat with another user on the network	**talk**
calculate a file's *checksum*	**sum**
clear the screen	**clear**
display a *column* from a sorted file	**cut**
strip *column*-formatting commands	**col**
combine presorted files with a common field	**join**
combine several files into a new file	**cat**
run *command* at specific time	**at**
run a series of *commands*	**batch**
time a *command*	**time, timex**
compare contents of two directories	**dircmp**
compare contents of two presorted files	**comm**

If you want to...	Use the UNIX command...
compare three files to see if they are different	**diff3**
compare two files and report on differing lines	**diff**
compare two files and return differing lines	**bdiff**
compare two files to see if they are different	**cmp**
compare two files and report differences and commonalties	**sdiff**
compile C programs	**cc**
compress a file	**compress, pack**
copy a file	**cat, cp**
copy files to and from networked remote systems	**rcp**
copy files to and from remote UNIX system	**uucp**
count the number of words in text file	**wc**
create a new text file	**cat**
change *current directory*	**cd**
stop a *current process*	**kill**
display *date* and time	**date**
change a file's *date* to the current date	**touch**
decode file after communications	**uudecode**
delete a file	**rm**
create a *directory*	**mkdir**
display disk space used by a *directory*	**du**
generate a *directory* listing	**ls**
change current working *directory*	**cd**

If you want to...	Use the UNIX command...
remove a *directory*	**rmdir**
return current working *directory*	**pwd**
compare the contents of two *directories*	**dircmp**
display free or total *disk space*	**df**
display *disk space* used by a directory	**du**
display a file	**cat, page**
display a file one screen at a time	**more**
display first ten lines of a file	**head**
display last ten lines of a file	**tail**
display packed files	**pcat**
edit a text file	**vi, ed**
send *electronic mail*	**mailx**
send return *electronic mail* when you're on vacation	**vacation**
notify you when *electronic mail* arrives	**notify**
encode file before communications	**uuencode**
encrypt a file	**crypt**
display or set *environment variables*	**env**
format *equations*	**eqn, neqn**
erase a file	**rm**
exit	**exit**
copy a *file*	**cat, cp**
create a new text *file*	**cat**
change a *file's* date to the current date	**touch**
display a *file*	**cat, page**
display a *file* one screen at a time	**more**
display first ten lines of a *file*	**head**

If you want to...	Use the UNIX command...
display last ten lines of a *file*	**tail**
edit a *file*	**vi, ed**
encrypt a *file*	**crypt**
erase a *file*	**rm**
find a *file*	**find**
format a structured *file*	**awk, nawk**
send output to *file* as well as screen	**tee**
change ownership of *file*	**chown**
move a *file* or multiple files	**mv**
display a column from a sorted *file*	**cut**
sort a *file*	**sort**
sort a structured *file*	**awk, nawk**
search a structured *file*	**awk, nawk, grep**
split a *file* into smaller files	**csplit, split**
determine *file* type	**file**
change *file-access permissions*	**chmod**
create or determine default *file-access permissions*	**umask**
append other *files* to an existing file	**cat**
combine presorted *files* with a common field	**join**
combine several *files* into a new file	**cat**
compare contents of two presorted *files*	**comm**
compare three *files* to see if they are different	**diff3**
compare two *files* and report on differing lines	**diff**

If you want to...	Use the UNIX command...
compare two *files* and return differing lines	**bdiff**
compare two *files* to see if they are different	**cmp**
display packed *files*	**pcat**
merge *files* side by side	**paste**
change group membership of *files*	**chgrp**
list *files*	**ls**
link *files*	**ln**
search for ASCII strings within binary *files*	**strings**
remove *files*	**rm**
find the *full filename*	**basename**
find a file	**find**
format equations	**eqn, neqn**
format tables	**tbl**
format text file	**newform**
format a structured file	**awk, nawk**
format text for laser printer	**troff**
format text for line printer	**nroff**
format text (right justify)	**fmt**
format text to specific width	**fold**
log in new *group*	**newgrp**
find what *groups* a user belongs to	**groups**
get *help*	**man, apropos, whatis**
display user *ID*	**id**
start *Korn shell*	**ksh**
insert *line numbers* in text file	**nl**

If you want to...	Use the UNIX command...
link files	**ln**
list files	**ls**
save a *log* of your current computing session	**script**
log in as another user	**su**
log in new group	**newgrp**
log in remote system	**rlogin, telnet**
log in system	**login**
print your *login name*	**logname**
print *logins* to other remote systems	**uulog**
log off system	**exit**
run a command even after you *log off* the system	**nohup**
show who is *logged on* the system	**who, rwho**
run a command at a *low priority*	**nice**
send electronic *mail*	**mailx**
send return electronic *mail* when you're on vacation	**vacation**
notify you when *mail* arrives	**notify**
perform *math* calculations	**bc, dc**
merge files side by side	**paste**
send *message* to all users logged on the system	**wall**
turn on/off the ability to receive *messages* from other users	**mesg**
move a file or multiple files	**mv**
display system *news*	**news**
show status of all machines on *network*	**ruptime**
run a command *nicely* (at a lower priority)	**nice**

If you want to...	Use the UNIX command...
send *output* to file as well as screen	**tee**
change *ownership* of file	**chown**
change group *ownership* of files	**chgrp**
pack a file	**compress, pack**
display *packed* files	**pcat**
set your *password*	**passwd**
pause before executing a command	**sleep**
print	**lp**
prepare a file for *printing*	**pr**
print a 10-character banner	**banner**
cancel *print* job	**cancel**
print jobs scheduled with **at** command	**atq**
show status of *print* requests	**lpstat**
start *print spooler*	**lpsched**
stop *print spooler*	**lpshut**
stop a current *process*	**kill**
show current *processes*	**ps**
quit	**exit**
schedule *recurring* tasks	**crontab**
start a remote shell on a *remote system*	**rsh**
copy files to and from *remote system*	**rcp, uucp, ftp**
log on *remote system*	**telnet, rlogin**
start a remote shell on a *remote system*	**rsh**
run a UNIX command on a *remote system*	**uux**
print logins to other *remote systems*	**uulog**
remove a directory	**rmdir**
remove files	**rm**

run a UNIX command on a remote system	**uux**
schedule personal events	**calendar**
schedule recurring tasks	**crontab**
search a structured file	**awk, nawk, grep**
search for text string	**egrep, grep, fgrep**
search and replace ASCII characters	**tr**
sort a file	**sort**
sort a structured file	**awk, nawk**
check *spelling* in text file	**spell**
split a file into smaller files	**csplit, split**
display to *standard output*	**echo**
show *status* of all machines on the network	**ruptime**
search for text *string*	**egrep, grep, fgrep**
strip column-formatting commands	**col**
strip formatting commands	**deroff**
return UNIX *system name*	**uname**
display *system news*	**news**
list *systems* that you can communicate with	**uuname**
format *tables*	**tbl**
set *tabs*	**tabs**
create a *tape* backup	**tar, cpio**
display *terminal* information	**tput**
display *terminal* options	**tty**
set *terminal* configuration	**stty**

UNIX in
Plain English

27

If you want to...	Use the UNIX command...
check spelling in *text* file	**spell**
format *text* file	**newform**
format *text* for laser printer	**troff**
format *text* for line printer	**nroff**
format *text* (right justify)	**fmt**
format *text* to specific width	**fold**
insert line numbers in *text* file	**nl**
create a new *text file*	**cat**
search for *text string*	**egrep, grep, fgrep**
display date and *time*	**date**
run command at specific *time*	**at**
time a command	**time, timex**
determine file *type*	**file**
uncompress a file	**uncompress**
unpack a file	**unpack**
display *user ID*	**id**
list *users*	**listusers**
display information about other *users* on the system	**who**
find information about other *users* on the system	**finger**
show status of *uucp requests*	**uustat**
send return mail when you're on *vacation*	**vacation**
force shell to *wait*	**wait**
write message to other user on the network	**write**
count the number of *words* in text file	**wc**
return current *working directory*	**pwd**

3

UNIX/DOS
Cross Reference

Old-time UNIX hacks may find it a heresy to include a DOS cross reference in a UNIX reference text. After all, isn't UNIX the greatest operating system ever created? There are a few good reasons why we included this section.

- Most computer users, whether or not they are using UNIX, have some familiarity with DOS. It's our experience that if a computer user is using one operating system at home, it probably is DOS on a PC clone. The personal computer made personal computing affordable for the masses. And, after all, DOS is one of the most popular operating systems on the face of the earth.

- Many UNIX users will be moving up from DOS. This is an unalterable fact of UNIX life. Many corporations are finding that DOS-based networks simply can't handle the large-scale computing chores handled rather effortlessly by a UNIX-based network.

- DOS has its roots in UNIX. The originators of DOS, Seattle Computer Works (*not* Microsoft, incidentally), patterned DOS after UNIX using many of the same commands (such as **cd** and **echo**) and maintaining the same file structure and philosophy (standard input/output plays a large role in DOS computing). Of course, this was many, many years ago, and both DOS and UNIX have changed quite a bit in response to differing computing needs. For instance, DOS focuses on disk utilities, such as CHKDSK and DISKCOPY; UNIX emphasizes networking, text-editing, and text-manipulation commands. Both operating systems changed in response to the folks who ended up using them. Single, stand-alone PC users are the biggest users of DOS, obviously, while UNIX's strengths are in the multiuser corporate and college worlds.

Don't worry if you're a DOS user and don't recognize all of the DOS commands in this list. Like UNIX, some older DOS commands have managed to hang in there despite their relative obscurity. It's safe to say that 99 percent of all DOS users have never even *heard* of the **CTTY** command, much less used it. And since this listing of DOS commands is current as of MS-DOS 6.0, there are many new commands (such as **MSAV**, which concerns an anti-virus utility) that may still be unfamiliar.

Not all DOS commands have a UNIX analog. Similarly, some UNIX commands simply have no parallel in the DOS world. In cases of DOS commands with no UNIX parallel, we note that situation. Not all of the commands are *perfectly* matched; in some cases, we listed the rough equivalent.

DOS command	UNIX command
APPEND	*None*
ASSIGN	*None*
ATTRIB	**chmod**
BACKUP	**cpio, tar**
BREAK	*None*
CALL	**exec**
CD	**cd**
CHCP	*None*
CHDIR	**cd**
CHKDSK	*None*
CHOICE	*None*
CLS	**clear**
COMMAND	**csh, sh**
COMP	**bdiff, cmp, diff, diff3, sdiff**
COPY	**cp**
CTTY	**stty**
DATE	**date**
DBLSPACE	*None*
DEFRAG	*None*
DEL	**rm**
DELTREE	**rm -r**
DIR	**ls**
DISKCOMP	*None*
DISKCOPY	*None*
DOSKEY	**history** (Korn and Bourne shells)
DOSSHELL	*None*
ECHO	**echo**
EDIT	**vi**

UNIX/DOS
Cross Reference

DOS command	UNIX command
EXIT	*None*
EXPAND	**uncompress, unpack**
FASTHELP	**apropos, man, whatis**
FASTOPEN	*None*
FC	**bdiff, cmp, diff, diff3, sdiff**
FDISK	*None*
FIND	**find**
FOR	**for** (shell command)
FORMAT	*None*
GOTO	**goto** (C shell)
GRAFTABL	*None*
GRAPHICS	*None*
HELP	**apropos, man, whatis**
IF	**if** (shell command)
INTERLNK	*None*
INTERSVR	*None*
JOIN	*None*
KEYB	*None*
LABEL	*None*
LOADFIX	*None*
LOADHIGH	*None* (thankfully)
MEM	*None*
MEMMAKER	*None*
MIRROR	*None*
MKDIR	**mkdir**
MODE	**stty, tty**
MORE	**more**
MOVE	**mv**

DOS command	UNIX command
MSAV	*None*
MSBACKUP	**cpio**, **tar**
MSD	*None*
NLSFUNC	*None*
PATH	**setenv PATH** (C shell), **setpath** (Bourne shell)
PAUSE	*None*
POWER	*None*
PRINT	**pr**
PROMPT	**PS1**
RECOVER	*None*
REM	**#**
RENAME	**move**
REPLACE	*None*
RESTORE	**cpio**, **tar**
RMDIR	**rmdir**
SET	**env**
SETVER	*None*
SHARE	*None*
SHIFT	*None*
SMARTDRV	*None*
SORT	**sort**
SUBST	*None*
SYS	*None*
TIME	**date**
TREE	*None*
TYPE	**more**, **page**
UNDELETE	*None* (unfortunately)

DOS command	UNIX command
UNFORMAT	*None*
VER	**uname**
VERIFY	*None*
VOL	*None*
VSAFE	*None*
XCOPY	**cp**

4

UNIX Commands
A to Z

Here is an alphabetical listing of the commands covered in Sections 5 and 6. This inventory does not include every available UNIX command—life's too short and we're too young to undertake such a task. Most UNIX users aren't going to use all the commands listed here, much less an additional set of commands whose obscurity is unrivaled only by its lack of usefulness in everyday computing chores.

This list was prepared for the majority of UNIX users who want to get on with their work and not let the operating system interfere with their chores. To that end, it represents the UNIX commands users are most likely to use.

Command	Section
apropos	General-Purpose Commands
at	System-Administration Commands
atq	System-Administration Commands
atrm	System-Administration Commands
awk	Text-Processing Command
banner	Printing Commands
basename	General-Purpose Commands
batch	System-Administration Commands
bc	General-Purpose Commands
bdiff	File-Manipulation Commands
cal	General-Purpose Commands
calendar	General-Purpose Commands
cancel	Printing Commands
cat	File-Manipulation Commands
cc	General-Purpose Commands
cd	File-Manipulation Commands
chgrp	System-Administration Commands
chmod	General-Purpose Commands
chown	File-Manipulation Commands
clear	General-Purpose Commands
cmp	File-Manipulation Commands
col	Text-Processing Commands
comm	File-Manipulation Commands
compress	File-Manipulation Commands
cp	File-Manipulation Commands
cpio	System-Administration Commands
crontab	System-Administration Commands
crypt	File-Manipulation Commands

Command	Section
csh	General-Purpose Commands
csplit	File-Manipulation Commands
ct	Communications Commands
cu	Communications Commands
cut	Text-Processing Commands
date	General-Purpose Commands
dc	General-Purpose Commands
deroff	Text-Processing Commands
df	General-Purpose Commands
diff	File-Manipulation Commands
diff3	File-Manipulation Commands
dircmp	File-Manipulation Commands
du	General-Purpose Commands
echo	General-Purpose Commands
ed	Text-Processing Commands
egrep	File-Manipulation Commands
env	General-Purpose Commands
eqn	Text-Processing Commands
exit	General-Purpose Commands
fgrep	File-Manipulation Commands
file	File-Manipulation Commands
find	File-Manipulation Commands
finger	General-Purpose Commands
fmt	Text-Processing Commands
fold	Text-Processing Commands
ftp	Communications Commands
grep	File-Manipulation Commands
groups	General-Purpose Commands

UNIX Commands
A to Z

Command	Section
head	File-Manipulation Commands
id	General-Purpose Commands
join	File-Manipulation Commands
kill	General-Purpose Commands
ksh	General-Purpose Commands
listusers	General-Purpose Commands
ln	File-Manipulation Commands
login	System-Administration Commands
logname	Communications Commands
lp	Printing Commands
lpsched	Printing Commands
lpshut	Printing Commands
lpstat	Printing Commands
ls	File-Manipulation Commands
mailx	Communications Commands
man	General-Purpose Commands
mesg	Communications Commands
mkdir	File-Manipulation Commands
more	File-Manipulation Commands
mv	File-Manipulation Commands
nawk	Text-Processing Commands
neqn	Text-Processing Commands
newform	Text-Processing Commands
newgrp	System-Administration Commands
news	General-Purpose Commands
nice	General-Purpose Commands
nl	Text-Processing Commands
nohup	General-Purpose Commands

Command	Section
notify	Communications Commands
nroff	Text-Processing Commands
pack	File-Manipulation Commands
page	File-Manipulation Commands
passwd	General-Purpose Commands
paste	Text-Processing Commands
pcat	File-Manipulation Commands
pr	Printing Commands
ps	General-Purpose Commands
pwd	General-Purpose Commands
rcp	Communications Commands
rlogin	Communications Commands
rm	File-Manipulation Commands
rmdir	File-Manipulation Commands
rsh	Communications Commands
ruptime	General-Purpose Commands
rwho	General-Purpose Commands
script	General-Purpose Commands
sdiff	File-Manipulation Commands
sh	General-Purpose Commands
shutdown	System-Administration Commands
sleep	General-Purpose Commands
sort	Text-Processing Commands
spell	Text-Processing Commands
split	File-Manipulation Commands
strings	File-Manipulation Commands
stty	System-Administration Commands
su	General-Purpose Commands

UNIX Commands
A to Z

Command	Section
sum	Communications Commands
tabs	Text-Processing Commands
tail	File-Manipulation Commands
talk	Communications Commands
tar	File-Manipulation Commands
tbl	Text-Processing Commands
tee	General-Purpose Commands
telnet	Communications Commands
time	General-Purpose Commands
timex	General-Purpose Commands
touch	File-Manipulation Commands
tput	System-Administration Commands
tr	Text-Processing Commands
troff	Text-Processing Commands
tty	System-Administration Commands
umask	General-Purpose Commands
uname	General-Purpose Commands
uncompress	File-Manipulation Commands
uniq	Text-Processing Commands
unpack	File-Manipulation Commands
uucp	Communications Commands
uudecode	Communications Commands
uuencode	Communications Commands
uulog	Communications Commands
uuname	Communications Commands
uustat	Communications Commands
uux	Communications Commands

Command	Section
vacation	Communications Commands
vi	Text-Processing Commands
wait	General-Purpose Commands
wall	Communications Commands
wc	Text-Processing Commands
whatis	General-Purpose Commands
who	General-Purpose Commands
write	Communications Commands

UNIX Commands
A to Z

5

UNIX Commands, Organized by Group

This section organizes UNIX commands by group and function. We think you'll find this method of organization best suited for your daily tasks; most people run across a problem and then try to solve it. This method of organization allows you to hone in on the general topic, and from there you can browse through the appropriate commands to find the one that best serves your needs.

The five categories are:

- General-Purpose Commands

- File-Manipulation Commands

- Text-Processing Commands

- Printing Commands

- Communication Commands

Each command's explanation follows the same structure. An initial line shows how you would use this command as part of a command line. For instance, some commands require you to list a filename, while others support various options. In the instances where you need to enter information specific to your circumstances—such as filenames and options—these variables are printed in *italics*.

Additional information includes the command's purpose (a short chunk of text, where commands are listed in **boldface**), an example (where appropriate; these are command lines that would be directly entered in your system), options, and related commands (where appropriate).

These commands have been tested with a wide range of UNIX systems (for a complete list, see the Introduction). We've tried to flag instances where a command may not be available on all systems. In addition, a few commands work differently depending on if you're using BSD UNIX (referred to as BSD in this section) or System V UNIX (referred to as SV), while others were newly introduced in System V Release 4 (referred to as SVR4).

General-Purpose Commands

These general-purpose commands are geared to the everyday tasks of UNIX usage and cover a wide variety of tasks.

apropos *keyword(s)*

PURPOSE

Returns information about the specified *keyword(s)* from the online manual pages. Not available on all systems.

EXAMPLE

```
$ apropos shell
```

OPTIONS

None.

RELATED COMMANDS

man
: Returns information from online manual pages.

whatis
: Returns information from online manual pages.

basename   Actual Filename

basename *pathname suffix*

PURPOSE

Returns just the actual filename when presented with a
pathname. If a suffix is specified, then the suffix will
also be removed. Generally, **basename** is used in shell
scripts and in other situations calling for command sub-
stitution.

EXAMPLE

```
$ basename
/usr/users/kevin/files/topics/1994/stuff
stuff
```

OPTIONS

None.

bc   Calculator

bc *options files*

PURPOSE

This calculator command supports a wide range of options and conditions. **bc** is also a language very similar to the C programming language.

After running the **bc** command, the command prompt disappears, and then keywords, symbols, and operations can be entered directly.

bc is an involved tool that's far too complicated for this introductory work, as there's a whole set of specialized instructions that are not even listed here, as you'll see from the short example. See the Bibliography for a list of UNIX tutorials that should cover **bc** in some form.

EXAMPLE

```
$ bc
scale=5
sqrt((66*6)/55)
2.6832
quit
```

OPTIONS

-c   Compiles the specified *filename*.

-l   Makes the math library available. (Note: When you invoke this option, you automatically set the scale to 20.)

COMMON INSTRUCTIONS

+	Addition.
-	Subtraction.
/	Division.
*	Multiplication.
%	Remainder.
^	Exponentiation.
sqrt(n)	Square root.
scale=n	Sets scale (after decimal point).
ibase=n	Sets input base (default is 10).
obase=x	Sets output base (default is 10).
define a(b)	Defines the function a with the argument b.
for, if, while	Statement keywords.

OTHER OPERATORS AND SYMBOLS

assignment	=+ =- =* =/ =^ =
relational	< <= > >= == !=
unary	- ++ —

OTHER SYMBOLS

/* */	Comment lines.
{}	Brackets statements.
[]	Array index.
text	Prints *text*.

General
Purpose

MATH-LIBRARY FUNCTIONS

s	Sine.
c	Cosine.
a	Arctangent.
e	Exponential; base e.
l	Natural logarithm.
j(*n*,*x*)	Bessel function.

RELATED COMMANDS

dc	Desk calculator.

cal *option*

PURPOSE

Displays the current month in calendar form. If a year is specified, then a 12-month calendar is printed. If a month and year are specified, then that specific month is printed.

Don't confuse the *cal* **command with the** *calendar* **command.**

N O T E

The *command cal 94* **displays the calendar for the year A.D. 94, not 1994. Also, the calendar is based on the British/American convention. Try** *cal 1752* **to see the jump to the Gregorian calendar.**

N O T E

EXAMPLES

```
cal
cal 11 1994
cal 1994
cal 1752
```

OPTIONS

month	Specific month, in numerical form.
year	Specific year.

Continued

RELATED COMMANDS

calendar   Sets up a personal calendar.

date   Displays current date and time.

calendar *option*

PURPOSE

This rudimentary personal organizer allows you to store events in a file named **calendar**. On the current day, the **calendar** command will scan the **calendar** file for all events occurring on that day. (Many users place the **calendar** commands in their startup files.) The events must be listed on one line, with the date in one of three formats:

```
11/12
Nov. 12
November 12
```

EXAMPLES

```
11/12   drinks with Eric
11/15   drinks with Eric
11/18   drinks with Eric
```

(This reminds the user of these important engagements when the **calendar** command is run on November 11, November 15, and November 18.)

OPTION

Privileged users can use this option to scan the system for files named **calendar** in login directories, automatically sending corresponding events from each file to the appropriate user.

General
Purpose

Continued

RELATED COMMANDS

cal   Returns a monthly or yearly calendar.

date   Displays current date and time.

 Don't confuse the *cal* command with the *calendar* command.

cc *options files*

PURPOSE

Compiles C language programs (source files, assembler source files, or preprocessed C source files).

EXAMPLE

```
$ cc -o hello hello.o
```

(This creates an executable file named **hello** from an object module named **hello.o**.)

OPTIONS

-c *filename*   Specifies the name of the file to compile, to generate a `.o` file.

-g   Generates debugging information.

-o *filename*   Specifies the name of the executable file to generate.

-O   Optimizes while compiling.

-l *library*   Links in the given library, e.g., `-lX11`.

There are literally dozens of options available for this command. Check your system documentation or online manual page for a full set.

chmod *option mode filename(s)*

PURPOSE

Changes the file-access permissions on a given file or files, or on the contents of an entire subdirectory. Only the owner of the file or a privileged user can change the mode of a file. There are two ways to change permissions: through symbolic or numeric form. The numeric form is used to set absolute permission values, while the symbolic form is used to set values relative to the current value.

To get the current permissions, use the **ls** command, which is covered elsewhere in this section.

EXAMPLE USING NUMERIC FORM

```
$ chmod 744 kevin.report
```

This example uses the **chmod** command on the file **kevin.report** to a permission status where the owner can read, write, and execute a file, while the file's specified group and all other users can read the file but cannot execute the file or write to it.

The value of *744* comes from adding the mode values found in the next section, "Modes." The lowest possible value is 000—which means no one can read, write, or execute the file—while the highest-possible value is 777—where everyone can read, write, and execute the file. Here's the exact arithmetic used to arrive at 744:

400   Owner has read permission.
200   Owner has write permission.
100   Owner has execute permission.

Continued

040	Group has read permission.
004	World has read permission.
———	
744	

The next time you run an **ls** command (using the long form, of course) on the file **kevin.report**, the permissions would be set as

```
rwxr--r--
```

MODES

The *mode* is an octal number in the following format:

Number	Meaning
400	Owner has read permission.
200	Owner has write permission.
100	Owner has execute permission.
040	Group has read permission.
020	Group has write permission.
010	Group has execute permission.
004	World has read permission.
002	World has write permission.
001	World has execute permission.

Add together the numbers for the permissions you want. For example, 423 means that you, the user, can read the file, users in your group can write the file and the rest of the world can write and execute the file. (Note that you usually need read permission to execute a file.)

General Purpose

Continued

THE SYMBOLIC FORM

When setting permissions in this manner, the modes are entered in symbolic form, but the structure of the command remains the same. Instead of using numerals in the mode field, you'd use one of the following symbols:

Symbol	Meaning
u	User (who actually owns the file).
g	Group.
o	Other.
all	All (this is the default).
+	Adds a permission to the current permissions.
-	Removes a permission from the current permissions.
=	Assign an absolute permission irrespective of the current permission.
r	Read.
w	Write.
x	Execute.
l	Mandatory lock during access.

You can set more than one mode at a time, making sure that the settings are separated by a comma (with no spaces on either side of it). In addition, you can set permissions for more than one set of users in the same mode statement, as shown in the following examples.

Continued

EXAMPLES USING SYMBOLIC FORM

```
$ chmod u+x kevin.report
```

(This allows the owner of the file **kevin.report** to execute the file.)

```
$ chmod u-x kevin.report
```

(This removes the ability of the owner of the file **kevin.report** to execute the file.)

```
$ chmod u+x,go-w file.report
```

(This allows the owner of the file **kevin.report** to execute the file, while removing the permissions of the group and all other users to write to the file.)

OPTION

-R   Recursively changes through subdirectories and files.

RELATED COMMANDS

chgrp   Changes group membership.

chown   Changes file ownership.

newgrp   Changes to a new working group.

General
Purpose

clear

PURPOSE

Clears the screen.

EXAMPLE

```
$ clear
```

csh

PURPOSE

Starts the C shell, one of many UNIX command-line interfaces. See Section 7, "Shell Commands and Variables," for more information.

date *option +format*
date *option string* **(for privileged users)**

PURPOSE

Displays current date in a wide variety of formats (as the list of options indicates). Or, for those with privileged status, the **date** command can be used to set the system date and time.

EXAMPLES

```
$ date
```

(This returns the current date and time.)

```
$ date -u
```

(This returns the date and time in universal time, or Greenwich Mean Time.)

```
$ date +%A
```

(This returns the date and time with the day of the week spelled out.)

```
$ date 1115063094
```

(This sets the date and time to November 15, 6:30 a.m., 1994. Only privileged users can change the system date and time.)

OPTION

-u   Returns the date and time in universal time, or Greenwich Mean Time (GMT).

Continued

OPTIONS (PRIVILEGED USERS)

-a[-]s,f   Adjusts the time by seconds (s) or frac-
                    tions of seconds (f). The default is to
                    adjust the time forward; use - to adjust
                    the time backward.

[MMdd]hhmm[yy]]   Changes the date and time (using
                    month, day, hour, minute, and year).

FORMATS

%a   Day of the week abbreviated (Sun, Mon,
              et al.).

%A   Day of the week spelled out (Sunday,
              Monday, et al.).

%b   Month abbreviated (Jan, Feb, et al.); same
              as %h.

%B   Month spelled out (January, February,
              et al.).

%c   Date and time for a particular country.

%d   Day of the month in two digits (01–31).

%D   Date returned in mm/dd/yy format.

%e   Day of the month as numeral (1–31).

%h   Month abbreviated (Jan, Feb, et al.); same
              as %b.

%H   Hours returned in military time (00–24).

%I   Hours returned in nonmilitary time (0–12).

%j   Day returned in Julian date (001–365).

Continued

%m	Month returned as a number (01 for January, 02 for February, et al.).
%M	Minutes (0–59).
%n	Inserts a newline.
%p	Time of day indicated (AM or PM).
%S	Seconds (0–59).
%t	Inserts a tab.
%T	Time in *hh:mm:ss* format.
%U	Week returned as a number (0–51), with week starting on Sunday.
%w	Day of the week as a number (0 for Sunday, 1 for Monday, et al.).
%W	Week returned as a number (0–51), with week starting on a Monday.
%x	Country-specific time format.
%X	Country-specific date format.
%y	Year returned in two digits (94).
%Y	Year returned in four digits (1994).
%Z	Time zone.

dc — Desk Calculator

dc *file*

PURPOSE

Performs arbitrary-precision integer arithmetic, either from commands contained in a file or from keyboard input. Normally this command is not used on its own. The **bc** command acts as a friendly front end to the **dc** command, as the **dc** command works as a Reverse Polish Notation calculator—commands and operators follow the numbers they affect. Since most people are not used to working in this format, they prefer working with the more straightforward **bc** calculator.

EXAMPLES

```
$ 7 10 * p
70
```

(This multiplies 7 by 10 and then prints the result.)

```
$ 27-p
```

(This subtracts 27 from the previous number.)

COMMANDS

+	Adds last number to previous number.
-	Subtracts last number from previous number.
*	Multiplies last number times previous number.
/	Divides last number into previous number.
c	Clears all values.
i	Changes input base.

Continued

k	Sets scale factor (number of digits after decimal).
o	Changes output base.
p	Prints current result.
q	Quits **dc**.
v	Finds the square root.

RELATED COMMAND

bc	Calculator.

df *options file_system_name*

PURPOSE

Displays information about the amount of free disk space on a file system or a file system specified by *file_system_name*. A series of options allows you to display the total amount of free space (in kilobytes or disk blocks) or the total disk space.

EXAMPLES

```
$ df
```

(This returns the amount of free disk space in each directory.)

```
$ df -t
```

(This returns the amount of allocated space, as well as the free disk space.)

OPTIONS

-b   Displays the number of free disk space in kilobytes.

-e   Displays the number of free files. Not available on all systems.

-F *type*   Used to return information about unmounted file systems, specified by *type*. (A list of available types can be found in **/etc/vfstab** on some versions of UNIX.)

-g   Returns the entire **statvfs** structure for all unmounted file systems. (This command is new in SVR4.)

General
Purpose

Continued

-k	Prints the amount of allocation in kilobytes.
-l	Prints information only about local file systems.
-n	Displays the *type* of file system. Not available on all systems.
-t	Displays free space as well as allocated space. Not available on all systems.

RELATED COMMAND

du	Displays disk-space usage.

du *options files directories*

PURPOSE

Display how much disk space is used by a directory (and all its subdirectories) in blocks (usually 512 bytes each). The default is the current directory.

OPTIONS

-a	Displays information about all files, just not directories.
-r	Reports on files and directories **du** cannot open.
-s	Silent mode. Displays only totals.

RELATED COMMANDS

df	Displays disk free-space information.

General Purpose

echo *option string*

PURPOSE

Echoes text or values to standard output. Technically, **echo** exists in three forms: as a UNIX command (contained in **/bin/echo**), as a C shell command, and as a Bourne shell command. There are a few small differences. The C shell version does not support the **-n** option, nor does it support escape characters. However, the three are usually used interchangeably, and that is the approach used here.

EXAMPLES

```
$ echo "Good morning!"
```

(This would print the string *Good morning!* to the screen.)

```
$ echo "This is a test" | lp
```

(This would print the line *This is a test* to the line printer.)

OPTION

-n   Does not end the output with a newline. (This does not apply to the C shell version.)

CONTROL CHARACTERS

\b   Backspace.

\c   No newline.

Continued

\f	Form feed.
\n	Newline.
\r	Carriage return.
\t	Tab.
\v	Vertical tab.
****	Backslash.
n	ASCII code of any character.

General
Purpose

env *option [variable=value] command*

PURPOSE

Displays the current user environment variables with their values or makes changes to environment variables. The term *environment* refers to a variety of variable settings used by the command shell, including the login directory, default shell, login name, terminal type, and command path. When you change these settings, you are said to be changing the *environment*. This command works differently in the C shell. See Section 7, "Shell Commands and Variables," for more information.

EXAMPLES

$ env SHELL=/bin/csh

(This sets your default shell to the C shell.)

$ env HOME=/usr/users/kevin/notes

(This sets your home directory to /usr/users/kevin/notes.)

OPTION

-               Ignores the current environment variable.

exit   Exit Session

exit

PURPOSE

Quits the current session. This is actually a shell command, with differing options based on the shell version.

finger Find Information on Users

finger *options user(s)*

PURPOSE

Returns information about users with accounts on the system: username, full name, terminal, terminal access, time of login, and phone number. In addition, **finger** grabs information from the user's login shell, **.plan** file, and **.project** file. Information is returned in long display or short display.

The **finger** command searches for information based on a specific username or general first and last names. For instance, a search of the name of *smith* on a large system will probably yield quite a few responses. The use of the **finger** command with no username will return a list of all users currently logged on the system.

EXAMPLE

```
$ finger erc
Login name: erc          In real life: Eric Johnson
(612) 555-5555
Directory:/home/erc          Shell:/usr/bin/ksh
Last login Wed Nov 10 12:14:45 on term/07
Project: X Window Programming
erc        term/07      Nov 11 19:45
```

Continued

OPTIONS

-b	Long display, without information about home directory and shell.
-f	Short display, sans header.
-h	Long display, without information gleaned from the **.project** file.
-i	Shows "idle" status: username, terminal, time of login, and idle lines.
-l	Long display.
-m	Matches the username exactly, without searching for first or last names.
-p	Long display, without information gleaned from the **.plan** file.
-q	Quick display of username, terminal, and time of login, without searching for first or last names.
-s	Short format.
-w	Short format, without the user's first name.

RELATED COMMAND

who	Displays or changes usernames.

General
Purpose

groups   Groups

groups *user*

PURPOSE

Returns a list of the groups a *user* belongs to (the default is a listing of your groups).

RELATED COMMANDS

chgrp   Changes group.

newgrp   Changes group.

id *option*

PURPOSE

Displays your user ID and username, as well as your group ID and groupname.

OPTION

-a   Displays all groups.

RELATED COMMANDS

logname   Displays logname.

who   Displays users.

General
Purpose

kill *options PID*

PURPOSE

Kills a current process (specified by a PID, and returned by the **ps** command), as long as you own the process or are a privileged user. This command is also built into the Korn, Bourne, and C shells, although there are slight differences.

OPTIONS

-l	Lists the signal names.
-signal	The *signal* can be a number (returned by **ps -f**) or a name (returned by **kill -l**).

RELATED COMMAND

ps	Process status.

ksh

PURPOSE

Starts the Korn shell, one of UNIX's many command-line interfaces. See Section 7, "Shell Commands and Variables," for more information.

listusers   List Users

listusers *options*

PURPOSE

Returns a listing of usernames and IDs. Not available on all systems.

OPTIONS

-g *groupname* Returns members of *groupname*.

-l *login*   Returns list of users with the name *login*.

man *command*

PURPOSE

Displays the online manual page for a command. There's actually a lot more to this command, but most of it involves either Solaris 2.0 or advanced options geared toward more experienced users. If you want more information about the command specific to your system, use the **man man** command.

RELATED COMMANDS

apropos   Returns information for a specific keyword.

whatis   Returns information from online manual pages.

General
Purpose

news   Display System Messages

news *options newsitem(s)*

PURPOSE

Displays all news items distributed systemwide. These items are usually stored in **/usr/news** or **/var/news** and set up by the system administrator.

OPTIONS

-a	Displays all of the news items.
-n	Displays the names of all of the news items.
-s	Displays a count of all of the news items.

nice   Run Nicely

nice *option command arguments*

PURPOSE

Runs a command nicely, by giving it a very low priority. This is used for involved commands that can be run over a period of some time (such as over lunch), without causing you any inconvenience.

OPTION

-n   Specifies *n* as the decrement in priority. The default is 10.

nohup   No Hangups

nohup *command arguments* &

PURPOSE

Keeps a command running even if you log off the system.

passwd   Password

passwd *options*
passwd *options user* **(privileged users)**

PURPOSE

Sets the user's password.

OPTIONS

-s   Displays current password information:

user	Username.
status	Password status: **NP** (no password), **PS** (password), or **LK** (locked).
mm/dd/yy	Date when last changed.
min	Minimum number of days before password must be changed.
max	Maximum number of days before password must be changed.
notice	Number of days before you are given notice that your password must be changed.

OPTIONS (PRIVILEGED USERS)

-a   Displays password information for all users.

-d   Stops prompting user for password.

-f   Forces user to change password.

Continued

-l	Locks user password.
-n	Sets number of days that must pass before user can rechange password.
-w	Sets number of days before user is warned that the password expires.
-x	Sets number of days before password expires.

RELATED COMMAND

login   Login system.

ps *options*

PURPOSE

Returns the status of all current processes. When used by itself, **ps** returns basic information about a process by **PID** (process ID), **TTY**, **TIME**, and **COMMAND**. A rather long list of options allows you to find any additional information you might need more effectively. In BSD UNIX, the options are different; for instance, use **ps -aux** instead of **ps -ef**.

OPTIONS

-a	Displays all processes, except group leaders and those not controlled by a terminal.
-c	Displays information about scheduler priorities.
-d	Displays all processes, except group leaders.
-e	Displays information on every process.
-f	Displays full information about processes, including **UID**, **PID**, **PPID**, **C**, **STIME**, **TTY**, **TIME**, and **COMMAND**.
-g *list*	Displays processes for *list* of group leader IDs.
-j	Displays session and process group IDs.
-l	Displays a long listing, which includes such information as priorities set with the **nice** command—and much, much more.
-p *list*	Displays processes whose process IDs are contained in *list*.

General Purpose

Continued

-s *list*	Displays processes whose session leaders are contained in *list*.
-t *list*	Displays processes whose terminals are contained in *list*.
-u *list*	Displays processes whose users are contained in *list*.

RELATED COMMANDS

kill	Kills a process.
nice	Runs command at lower priority.

pwd   Print Working Directory

pwd

PURPOSE

Returns the current working directory.

OPTIONS

None.

RELATED COMMAND

cd   Changes directory.

ruptime   List Uptime

ruptime *options*

PURPOSE

Shows the status of all machines connected to the network. The resulting table shows the name of each host, whether the host is up or down, the amount of time it has been up or down, the number of users on the host, and the average load for that machine.

OPTIONS

-a	Includes all users, even those whose machines have been idle for more than an hour.
-l	Sorts by load.
-r	Reverses sort order.
-t	Sorts by uptime.
-u	Sorts by number of users.

rwho   Remote Who

rwho *option*

PURPOSE

Shows who is logged on all machines on the network.

OPTION

-a   Include all users, even those whose
                machines have been idle for more than
                an hour.

RELATED COMMAND

who   Users logged on the network.

script — Log Session

script *option filename*

PURPOSE

Saves a copy of your current computing session. (Actually, this starts a new session and logs it.) The default storage file is *typescript*, although you can change that on the command line. **Script** saves all characters that appear on your screen, including control and escape characters. The recording ends when you type **exit** or press **Ctrl-D** to end the session.

OPTION

-a   Appends output to the new *filename.*

sh

PURPOSE

Starts the Bourne shell. See Section 7, "Shell Commands and Variables," for more information.

sleep   Suspends Session

sleep *seconds*

PURPOSE

Suspends the system for a specified number of seconds before running another command. This command is handy when working with shell scripts.

RELATED COMMAND

wait   Waits for the completion of a process.

su   Substitute User

su *option user shell_args*

PURPOSE

Allows you to become another user without logging on
and off the system, suspending your current shell while
logging you in as the substitute user. The most common
use of **su** is to become temporarily the superuser to perform privileged administrative commands.

EXAMPLE

If you wanted to log in as **kevin** (which is an experience
every person should have in their lifetime) while already
logged in the system as **erc**, you would enter the following:

```
$ su kevin
```

The system would then prompt you for the password for
user *kevin*.

OPTION

-               Fully becomes the substitute user by adopt-
                ing the environment.

General
Purpose

RELATED COMMAND

login   Login system.

95

tee   Split Standard Output

tee *options file(s)*

PURPOSE

Sends standard output to a specified file, in addition to displaying the output on the screen. Without the use of **tee**, there's no way to redirect output from a command *both* to the screen and to a file, or to two separate commands. This command is never used on its own but rather as part of a longer command line.

EXAMPLES

```
$ spell textfile | tee badwords
```

(This runs the **spell** command on the file **textfile**, sending the output to a file named **badwords**.)

```
$ ls | tee textfile | wc
```

(This runs the **ls** command to generate a directory listing, sending the output to **tee**, which writes the listing to the file **textfile** and also sends the listing to the **wc** command, which displays a count of the lines, words, and bytes in the listing.)

OPTIONS

-a	Appends output to *file(s)*.
-i	Ignores system interrupts.

time *command*

PURPOSE

Runs a specified command and reports back on the time it took to run the command (elapsed time, user time, system time) in seconds. An expanded version, **timex**, is available on most UNIX systems.

EXAMPLE

```
$ time ls
```

(This runs the **ls** command, which generates a directory listing; **time** then prints the time it took to run **ls**.)

OPTIONS

None.

RELATED COMMAND

timex　　　　Displays time for running a command.

timex   Time a Command

timex *options command*

PURPOSE

Runs a specified command and reports back on the time it took to run the command (elapsed time, user time, system time) in seconds, with options for returning the number of blocks read and written, system activity, and other accounting information. This command is an expanded version of the **time** command.

OPTIONS

-o   Shows number of blocks used and characters transferred.

-p *suboptions*   Returns process activity for *command* though one or more of the suboptions:

     -f   Shows fork/exit flag and exit status.

     -h   Shows "hog" factor: CPU time divided by elapsed time.

     -k   Shows kcore time in minutes.

     -m   Shows mean core size (default).

     -r   Shows CPU use comparisons.

     -t   Shows CPU and system times.

-s   Returns total system activity while *command* is run.

RELATED COMMAND

time   Displays time for running a command.

umask User's File-Permission Mask

umask *values*

PURPOSE

Creates or returns the current value of the file-creation mask, which determines default values for new files. This value, also known as permissions, determines who has access to files and directories on the system. **umask** sets the default permissions for new files; you change the permissions for an existing file with **chmod**. On its own, **umask** returns the current default value.

However, **umask** uses a different method of specifying permissions—by numbers rather than symbols:

Umask number	File permission	Directory permission
0	rw-	rwx
1	rw-	rw-
2	r--	r-x
3	r--	r--
4	-w-	-wx
5	-w-	-w-
6	---	--x
7	---	---

EXAMPLE

```
$ umask 137
```

(This results in a file permission of -rw-r------.)

RELATED COMMAND

chmod   Changes permissions.

General
Purpose

99

uname   UNIX Name

uname *options*

PURPOSE

Returns the UNIX system name. On BSD systems, you'll have the **hostname** command instead.

 Do not confuse the *uname* **command with the** *uuname* **command.**

N O T E

EXAMPLE

```
$ uname -a
Sun OS eric 5.3 Generic sun4M sparc
```

OPTIONS

-a	Reports all information (the sum of all other options).
-m	Returns the hardware name.
-n	Returns the node name.
-p	Returns the processor type.
-r	Returns the operating-system release.
-s	Returns the system name.
-v	Returns the operating-system version.

wait   Wait for Job to Complete

wait *ID*

PURPOSE

Forces your shell to wait until background processes are completed before starting a new process.

OPTION

ID   Job-process ID.

RELATED COMMANDS

ps   Lists job processes.

sleep   Suspends execution.

whatis *command*

PURPOSE

Looks up the online manual page for *command* and presents a one-line summary.

RELATED COMMANDS

apropos	Returns help information about command.
man	Online manual pages.

who *options file*

PURPOSE

Displays the names and other information about users logged on the system.

OPTIONS

am I	Displays who you are (your system name).
-a	Uses all options listed here.
-b	Returns the last time and date the system was booted.
-d	Returns expired processes.
-H	Inserts column headings.
-l	Returns lines available for login.
-n*n*	Displays *n* users per line.
-p	Returns processes started by **init** that are still active.
-q	Quick who; displays only usernames.
-r	Returns run level.
-s	Returns name, line, and time fields (default).
-t	Returns the last time the system clock was updated with **clock**.
-T	Returns the state of each terminal:
	+ Any user can write to the terminal.

General
Purpose

Continued

-	Only system administrator can write to the terminal.
?	Error with the terminal.
-u	Returns terminal usage in idle time.

RELATED COMMANDS

date	Display date and time.
login	Login system.
mesg	Sets terminal access.
rwho	Remote who.

File-Manipulation Commands

These commands help you in working with UNIX directories and files.

bdiff   List Differences in Files

bdiff *file1 file2 options*

PURPOSE

Compares two files and reports on the differing lines. This command actually invokes the **diff** command after dividing a file into manageable chunks, and it works best with text files.

EXAMPLE

```
$ bdiff kevin.memo kevin.memo.alt
1c1
< Dear Mr. Johnson:
- - -
> Dear Scumbag:
```

OPTIONS

-n   Divides the files into segments *n* lines long. This affects the values returned regarding specific differing lines, as the example shows.

-s   Suppresses error messages.

Continued

RELATED COMMANDS

cmp   Compares two files and tells you if the files are different.

diff   Compares files and reports *all* differing lines.

diff3   Compares three files.

sdiff   Compares files side by side.

cat *options file(s)*

PURPOSE

Performs several frequently used chores:

- Combines several files into a new file (using the > operator).

- Appends other files to an existing file (using the >> operator).

- Displays a file when no operators are specified.

- Copies a file to a new name (using the > operator).

- Creates a new text file without the fuss of a text editor.

EXAMPLES

```
$ cat kevin.report
```

(This would display the contents of the file **kevin.report** nonstop on the screen.)

```
$ cat kevin.report kevin.memo
```

(This would display the contents of the files **kevin.report** and **kevin.memo** nonstop on the screen.)

Continued

```
$ cat kevin.report kevin.memo > kevin.words
```

(This would combine the contents of the files **kevin.report** and **kevin.memo** into a new file named **kevin.words**, in the order they appear on the command line.)

```
$ cat kevin.report.old > kevin.report.new
```

(This would copy the contents of **kevin.report.old** into the new file named **kevin.report.new**.)

```
$ cat > kevin.report.1994
```

(**Cat** creates a new file named **kevin.report.1994** and places all keyboard input into that file, halting input when the user presses **Ctrl-D**.)

```
$ cat kevin.report >> kevin.memo
```

(This appends contents of **kevin.report** to the end of the file **kevin.memo**.)

```
$ cat - >> kevin.report
```

(This appends keyboard input to the end of the file **kevin.report**.)

WARNING

If you're not careful about how you use **cat**, you could overwrite the contents of one file with keyboard entry or the contents of another file. For instance, the command:

```
$ cat - > kevin.report
```

replaces the current contents of **kevin.report** with keyboard input.

Continued

OPTIONS

-	Used as a substitute for a filename; allows for keyboard entry to be appended to an existing file. Press **Ctrl-D** to end the keyboard entry.
-s (SV)	Silent mode; suppresses information about nonexistent files.
-s (BSD)	Removes blank lines from the file.
-u	Output is unbuffered; default is buffered, which means that characters are displayed in blocks.
-v	Prints nonprinting characters, such as control characters, except for tabs, form feeds, and newlines.
-ve	Prints nonprinting characters, such as control characters, except for tabs and form feeds, while newlines appear as dollar signs ($).
-vt	Prints nonprinting characters, such as control characters, except for newlines, while tabs appear as ^I and form feeds as ^L.
-vet	Prints all nonprinting characters.

RELATED COMMANDS

cp	Copies files.
more	Displays files one screen at a time.
page	Displays files one page at a time.

cd   Change Directory

cd *directory*

PURPOSE

Changes current directory to a new directory. The command is actually a shell command but is usually treated as a regular UNIX command.

EXAMPLES

```
$ cd
```

(This returns you to your home directory.)

```
$ cd stuff
```

(This changes you to the subdirectory **stuff** and makes it the current directory.)

```
$ cd /usr/users/eric/private
```

(This changes your current directory to another directory named **/usr/users/eric/private**.)

```
$ cd ~/stuff/1994
```

(This moves you to a subdirectory within your home directory.)

```
$ cd ..
```

(This moves your current directory one level up in the directory hierarchy.)

File-Manipulation
Commands

Continued

OPTIONS

None.

RELATED COMMAND

pwd   Prints the name of the current directory.

 The *cd* command is also covered in Section 7, "Shell Commands and Variables."

NOTE

chown   Change Ownership

chown *options newowner file(s)*

PURPOSE

Changes the ownership of a given file or files to a new
owner. The new owner is either a user ID number or a
login name (these can be found in **/etc/passwd**). The
BSD version of this command also allows the group to
be changed.

EXAMPLE

```
$ chown kevin kevin.report
```

(This changes the ownership of the file **kevin.report** to
kevin.)

OPTIONS

-h   Changes the ownership of a symbolic link.
               Not available on all systems.

-R   Recursively changes through a subdirectory
               and symbolic links.

RELATED COMMANDS

chmod   Changes file-access permissions.

chgrp   Changes group membership.

newgrp   Changes to a new working group.

cmp   Compare Files

cmp *options file1 file2*

PURPOSE

Compares the contents of two files. If the files are different, then **cmp** returns the byte position and line number of the first difference between the two files. If there is no difference in the files, then **cmp** returns nothing. The **cmp** command works on all files, not just text files. Other similar commands, such as **diff** and **comm**, work only with text files.

EXAMPLE

```
$ cmp kevin.report kevin.memo
kevin.report kevin.memo differ: char 31, line 2
```

OPTIONS

-l   Displays the byte position and the differing characters for *all* differences within the file.

-s   Works silently, returning only the exit codes and not the instances of differences. The exit code is one of the following:

0   Files are identical.

1   Files are different.

2   One of the files is unreadable.

Continued

RELATED COMMANDS

comm   Compares files line by line.

diff   Compares files and returns differences.

sdiff   Compares files side by side.

comm *options file1 file2*

PURPOSE

Compares the contents of two presorted text files. The output is generated in three columns:

| Lines found in *file1* | Lines found in *file2* | Lines found in both files |

EXAMPLE

```
$ comm kevin.report kevin.memo
                                Dear Mr. Jones:
I am happy to       I am sad

                                to report that
                                your daughter,
                                Felicia, was
accepted             was rejected
```

OPTIONS

-1	Suppresses the printing of column 1.
-2	Suppresses the printing of column 2.
-3	Suppresses the printing of column 3.
-12	Prints only column 3.
-13	Prints only column 2.
-23	Prints only column 1.

Continued

RELATED COMMANDS

cmp	Compares files byte by byte.
diff	Compares files and returns differences.
sdiff	Compares files side by side.
sort	Sorts files.

compress   Compress Files

compress *options filename(s)*

PURPOSE

Compresses a file (or files), creating *filename.Z.*

OPTIONS

-b*n*   Changes the number of bits used in the compression process. The default is 16, and *n* can be set to a numeral between 9 and 16. The lower the setting, the larger the resulting compressed file.

-f   Compresses with no feedback.

-v   Returns information on how much the file was compressed.

RELATED COMMANDS

uncompress   Uncompresses a compressed file.

pack   Compresses a file or files.

unpack   Uncompresses a compressed file.

zcat   Uncompresses a compressed file.

cp *options sourcefile destinationfile*
cp *options file1 directory*
cp *options directory1 directory2*

PURPOSE

Copies the contents of one file into another file with a new name or into another directory, retaining the existing filename. It also copies the content of one directory into a new directory.

EXAMPLES

```
$ cp kevin.memo kevin.memo.old
```

(This copies the file **kevin.memo** into a new file called **kevin.memo.old**.)

```
$ cp kevin.memo /usr/users/kevin/old_junk
```

(This copies the file **kevin.memo** into the directory **/usr/users/kevin/old_junk**.)

```
$ cp -r /usr/users/kevin/usr/users/kevin/backup
```

(This copies the contents of the directory **/usr/users/kevin** into the new **directory /usr/users/kevin/backup**.)

OPTIONS

-i	Makes sure you don't overwrite existing file.
-p	Retains existing permissions. Not available on all systems.
-r	Copies entire directory.

File-Manipulation
Commands

119

Continued

RELATED COMMANDS

chgrp	Changes group membership.
chmod	Changes file-access permissions.
chown	Changes file ownership.
ln	Links files.
mv	Moves or renames a file.
rm	Removes a file.

crypt   Encrypt Files

crypt *password option < file > encryptedfile*

PURPOSE

Takes a text file and stores it in a new encrypted file. The command also allows you to read from an encrypted file, although UNIX text editors have the ability to read encrypted files. A file is encrypted in order to avoid unauthorized access.

You need the password both to encrypt a file and read an encrypted file, although the **-k** option allows you to set the password as an environmental variable, CRYPTKEY. The use of the **-k** option is highly frowned upon, since it lessens the security measures afforded by the **crypt** command.

 The *crypt* command is not supported in versions of UNIX destined for export, due to U.S. security laws.

N O T E

EXAMPLE

```
$ crypt < kevin.report > kevin.new.report
```

OPTION

-k   Uses the password set as an environmental variable, CRYPTKEY.

csplit   Split Files

csplit *options arguments*

PURPOSE

Splits a long file into a series of smaller files. When you set up the command line using **csplit**, you specify whether you want to divide up the file by size or by content—that is, through having **csplit** search for a specific expression.

The resulting files will begin with **xx**. For instance, the first file will be named **xx00**, the second named **xx01**, and so on. (However, you're limited to 100 files, so that the last file in this sequence would be named **xx99**.)

EXAMPLE

```
$ csplit -k gone_wind '/^Chapter/' {30}
```

(This splits the file **gone_wind** into 30 files, all beginning with the expression "Chapter.")

OPTIONS

-f*file*   Uses *file* instead of **xx** for the beginning of filenames. (For instance, with this option enabled as **-fthis**, the first filename would be **this00**.)

-k   Keeps files even though they may not meet command-line criteria.

-s   Suppresses character counts.

ARGUMENTS

/expr/   Creates a file that begins with the current
                    line through the line containing *expr*. You
                    can add a suffix that ends the file a line
                    before *expr* by appending *-1* or a line after
                    expr by appending *+1*.

%expr%   Same as */expr/*, except that no file is created
                    for the text prior to *expr*.

line   Creates a file that begins at the current line
                    and ends one *line* before line number line.
                    (Note: Some documentation refers to this
                    option as *num*. They are the same thing.)

{n}   Repeats the previous argument *n* times.
                    Unless you specify *n*, the command line
                    works only once.

RELATED COMMAND

split   Splits a file.

diff — List Differences in Files

diff *options diroptions file1 file2*

PURPOSE

Compares two files and reports differing lines. The results are clear: The line numbers of the differing lines are noted, while the offending line from *file1* is marked with < and the offending line from *file2* is marked with >. Three hyphens (---) separate the contents of the two files. This command works best with text files.

 Diff **cannot process large files; use** *bdiff* **in those situations.**

N O T E

EXAMPLE

```
$ diff erc.memo erc.memo.1112
1c1
< Dear Boss:
- - -
> Dear Mr. King:
4c4
< This idea should be nuked.
- - -
> —Eric
```

OPTIONS

-b	Ignores blanks at the end of line.
-c	Produces three lines of context for each difference.

124

diff	List Differences in Files

-C*n*	Produces *n* lines of context for each difference.
-D *def*	Combines *file1* and *file2*, using C preprocessor controls (*#ifdef*).
-e	Creates a script for the **ed** editor to make *file1* the same as *file2*.
-i	Ignores case.
-t	Expands tabs in output to spaces.
-w	Ignores spaces and tabs.

DIROPTIONS

-l	Long format with pagination by **pr**.
-r	Recursively runs **diff** for files in common subdirectories.
-s	Lists identical files.
-S*file*	Starts directory comparisons with *file*, ignoring files alphabetically listed before *file*.

RELATED COMMANDS

bdiff	Compares two files and returns the differences.
comm	Compares two files line by line.
cmp	Compares contents of two files.
diff3	Compares three files.
sdiff	Compares files side by side.

File-Manipulation Commands

diff3   List Differences in Files

diff3 *options file1 file2 file3*

PURPOSE

Compares three different files and reports the differences like **diff**. Returns one of the following codes:

     ==== All three files differ.
     ====**1** *file1* is different.
     ====**2** *file2* is different.
     ====**3** *file3* is different.

OPTIONS

-e	Creates an **ed** script that places differences between *file2* and *file3* into *file1*. Not available on all systems.
-E	Creates an **ed** script that places differences between *file2* and *file3* into *file1*, marking lines that differ in all three files with brackets.
-x	Creates an **ed** script that places differences between all three files.
-X	Creates an **ed** script that places differences between all three files, marking lines that differ in all three files with brackets. Not available on all systems.
-3	Creates an **ed** script that places differences between *file1* and *file3* into *file1*.

Continued

RELATED COMMANDS

bdiff	Compares two files and returns the differences.
cmp	Compares contents of two files.
comm	Compares two files line by line.
diff	Compares two files.
sdiff	Compares files side by side.

File-Manipulation
Commands

dircmp   Directory Compare

dircmp *options directory1 directory2*

PURPOSE

Compares the contents of two directories and returns information on how the directories differ, in the form of files found in the first directory, files found in the second directory, and files common to both directories.

OPTIONS

-d	Compares pairs of common files using the **diff** command.
-s	Suppresses information about identical files.
-w*n*	Changes the width of the output line to *n* characters; the default is 72.

RELATED COMMANDS

bdiff	Compares two files and returns the differences.
diff	Compares two files.
sdiff	Compares files side by side.

egrep   Search Files

egrep *options pattern file(s)*

PURPOSE

Searches for text (referred to as *patterns* or *expressions*) in a file or multiple files, displaying the results of the search. For instance, you could search for the strings *Spacely Sprockets* and *Jetson Enterprises* in multiple files.

Egrep is related to the commands **grep** and **fgrep**. It is considered the most powerful of the three, as it allows for the searching of multiple strings. In addition, **egrep** allows matching from a file containing a series of expressions. It is also considered to be the fastest of the three.

EXAMPLE

```
$ egrep "Spacely Sprockets|Jetson Enterprises" *
memo.112: This proposal from Spacely Sprockets
e.doc.93: A representative of Jetson Enterprises
```

(This searches all the files in the current directory—as indicated by the wildcard asterisk [*]—for the strings *Spacely Sprockets* and *Jetson Enterprises*.)

OPTIONS

-b   Returns block number of matched line.

-c   Returns only the number of matches, without quoting the text.

-e *string*   Used to search for *string* beginning with a hyphen (-).

File-Manipulation
Commands

Continued

-f *file*	Takes expressions from file *file*.
-h	Returns only matched text with no reference to filenames. Not available on all systems.
-i	Ignores case.
-l	Returns only file names containing a match, without quoting the text.
-n	Returns line number of matched text, as well as the text itself.
-v	Returns lines that do *not* match the text.

RELATED COMMANDS

diff	Compares two files.
fgrep	Searches for text in files.
grep	Searches for text in files.
sdiff	Compares files side by side.

fgrep   Fast Grep

fgrep *options pattern file(s)*

PURPOSE

Searches for text (referred to as *patterns* or *expressions*) in a file or multiple files, displaying the results of the search. For instance, you could search for the strings *Spacely Sprockets* and *Jetson Enterprises* in multiple files. **Fgrep** searches only for literal text strings. It will not search for expressions. **Fgrep** is related to the commands **grep** and **egrep**.

EXAMPLES

```
$ egrep "Spacely Sprockets|Jetson Enterprises" *
memo.112: This proposal from Spacely Sprockets
e.doc.93: A representative of Jetson Enterprises
```

(This searches all the files in the current directory—as indicated by the wildcard asterisk [*]—for the strings *Spacely Sprockets* and *Jetson Enterprises*.)

OPTIONS

-b   Returns block number of matched line.

-c   Returns only the number of matches, without quoting the text.

-e *string*   Used to search for *string* beginning with a hyphen (-).

-f *file*   Takes expressions from file *file*.

Continued

-h	Returns only matched text with no reference to filenames.
-i	Ignores case.
-l	Returns only filenames containing a match, without quoting the text.
-n	Returns line number of matched text, as well as the text itself.
-v	Returns lines that do *not* match the text.
-x	Returns a line only if the *string* matches an entire line.

RELATED COMMANDS

diff	Compares two files.
egrep	Searches for text in files.
grep	Searches for text in files.
sdiff	Compares files side by side.

file *options filename*

PURPOSE

Describes file type of given file. If needed, **file** will check the magic file (**/etc/magic**) for file types.

The information returned by *file* **is not always correct. However,** *file* **is best at detecting text files, shell scripts, PostScript files, and UNIX commands.**

WARNING

OPTIONS

-c	Checks the magic file.
-f*list*	Runs the **file** command on the filenames contained in the file **list**.
-h	Ignores symbolic links.
-m*file*	Uses *file* as the magic file, not **/etc/magic**.

File-Manipulation
Commands

find   Find Files

find *pathname(s) condition(s)*

PURPOSE

Finds a file. Of course, it's not *quite* that simple—you enter as many conditions as you want (relating to when the file was created, when it was last accessed, what links are present, and so on, as you'll see when you review the available conditions).

EXAMPLES

```
$ find / -ctime -2 -print
```

(This returns all the files on the entire file system that have been changed fewer than two days ago.)

```
$ file $HOME -name '*memo' -print
```

(This returns all the files in your home directory that end with the string *memo*.)

OPTIONS

-atime *days*   Finds files that were accessed:
                        +d   more than *d* days ago.
                        d   exactly *d* days ago.
                        -d   fewer than *d* days ago.

-ctime *days*   Finds files that were changed:
                        +d   more than *d* days ago.
                        d   exactly *d* days ago.
                        -d   fewer than *d* days ago.

-exec *command* { } \; Runs UNIX *command* after a file is found.

Continued

-follow	Follows symbolic links and the associated directories.
-fstype *type*	Finds files of a specific file *type*.
-group *group*	Finds files belonging to group *group*, which can be a name or ID.
-inum *num*	Finds a file with an inode number of *num*.
-links *links*	Finds files with: *+l* more than *l* links. *l* exactly *l* links. *-l* fewer than *l* links.
-local	Search for files on the local file system.
-mtime *days*	Finds files that were modified: *+d* more than *d* days ago. *d* exactly *d* days ago. *-d* fewer than *d* days ago.
-name *file*	Finds a file named *file*.
-newer *filename*	Returns all files that have been modified more recently than *filename*.
-nogroup	Finds files owned by a group not listed in **/etc/group**.
-nouser	Finds files owned by a user not listed in **/etc/passwd**.
-ok *command* **{ } \;**	Runs UNIX *command* after a file is found, verifying the action with the user.
-perms *nnn*	Matches specified file permissions (such as **rwx**).
-print	Prints the results of the search to the screen. This option is mandatory, if you want to see the results of your search.

Continued

-size _blocks_ [_chars_]   Finds a file that is _blocks_ blocks large, or _chars_ characters large.

-type _t_   Returns names of files of type _t_. Type _t_ can be **b** (block special file), **c** (character special file), **d** (directory), **f** (plain file), **l** (symbolic link), or **p** (pipe).

-user _user_   Matches files belonging to a user, specified by name or ID.

-xdev   Search for files on the same file system as the specified _pathname_. (Only for BSD systems.)

LOGICAL SELECTORS

-a   and

-o   or

\!   not

\(...\)   group together

grep *options pattern file(s)*

PURPOSE

Searches for text (referred to as *patterns* or *expressions*) in a file or multiple files, displaying the results of the search. For instance, you could search for the string *Spacely Sprockets* in multiple files.

Grep is related to the commands **fgrep** and **egrep**. Of the three, **grep** supports the fewest options and is considered to be the slowest of the three.

EXAMPLES

```
$ grep "Spacely Sprockets" *
memo.1112: This proposal from Spacely Sprockets
```

(This searches all the files in the current directory—as indicated by the wildcard asterisk [*]—for the string *Spacely Sprockets.*)

OPTIONS

-b	Returns block number of matched line. Not available on all systems.
-c	Returns only the number of matches, without quoting the text.
-h	Returns only matched text with no reference to filenames. Not available on all systems.
-i	Ignores case.

File-Manipulation
Commands

Continued

-l	Returns only filenames containing a match, without quoting the text.
-n	Returns line number of matched text, as well as the text itself.
-s	Suppresses error messages.
-v	Returns lines that do *not* match the text.

RELATED COMMANDS

diff	Compares two files.
egrep	Searches for text in files.
fgrep	Searches for text in files.
sdiff	Compares files side by side.

head ···· Display Top of File

head *option file(s)*

PURPOSE

Displays the beginning of a file. The default is 10 lines.

OPTION

-*n*   Specifies the number of lines to display. The default is 10 lines.

RELATED COMMAND

tail   Displays end of file.

join *options file1 file2*

PURPOSE

Joins together two presorted files that have a common
key field. Only lines containing the key field will be
joined.

EXAMPLE

```
$ cat workers
Eric      286    erc
Geisha    280    geisha
Kevin     279    kevin

$ cat workers.1
Eric      8      555-6674
Geisha    10     555-4221
Kevin     2      555-1112

join workers workers.1 > workers.2

cat workers.2
Eric      286    erc      8     555-6674
Geisha    280    geisha   10    555-4221
Kevin     279    kevin    2     555-1112
```

OPTIONS

-a*filename*	Lists lines in *filename* that cannot be joined. If *filename* is now specified, unjoinable lines from both files are listed.
-e *string*	Replaces empty fields in output with *string*.
-j*filename* ***m***	Joins on the *m*th field of file *filename* (or both if *filename* is not specified).
-o*field*	Output contains fields specified by field number *field*.
-t*char*	*Char* will be used as a field separator, instead of the default.

RELATED COMMANDS

awk	Text-processing language.
comm	Compares files line by line.
cut	Cuts fields.
sort	Sorts files.

File-Manipulation
Commands

ln options originalfile linkfile
ln options file(s) directory

PURPOSE

Links two or more files. In essence, this allows the same file to be accessed under different names. No matter how many names exist, there's still only one file. The **ln** command also creates linked files with the same name in different directories.

You may want to create *symbolic* links, since these links can occur across file systems, and they're easier to keep track of with the **ls** command.

Don't reverse the file order with this command, or you can inadvertently trash good files. Remember that *the first file is the original.* **The second file names the link. The link then point back at the original file.**

WARNING

EXAMPLES

```
$ ln kevin eric
```

(This creates a link named **eric** to the file **kevin**.)

```
$ ln kevin /usr/users/kevin/misc
```

(This creates a link to **kevin** in **/usr/users/kevin/misc**. The linked file will also be named **kevin**.)

Continued

OPTIONS

-f	Forces linking—that is, do not ask for confirmations.
-n	Does not overwrite an existing file.
-s	Creates a symbolic link.

RELATED COMMANDS

chmod	Changes file-access permissions.
chown	Changes file ownership.
cp	Copies files.
ls	Lists files.
mv	Moves files.

File-Manipulation
Commands

ls *options names*

PURPOSE

Lists the contents of the specified directory. If no directory is specified, the contents of the current directory are listed. This is both one of the simplest (conceptually, there's nothing more simple than returning the contents of a directory) and complex (witness the presence of 23 options!) commands within the UNIX operating system. Of course, out of the 23 options, not all are equal; you'll use **-F** and **-l** quite a bit, while chances are you won't find much use for **-u** or **-c**.

EXAMPLES

```
$ ls
data       figures      misc    newdata     personnel
expenses   financials
```

(This returns a listing of the files in the current directory.)

```
$ ls newdata
newdata
```

(This confirms that the file **newdata** is contained in the current directory.)

```
$ ls god
god not found
```

(This searches for a specific file, which is not in the current directory.)

```
$ ls -a
   .  ..  .mailrc   .profile  data  financials  misc
   newdata          personnel
```

Continued

(This lists all files, including hidden files, which begin with a period [.].)

OPTIONS

-1	Lists one item per line.
-a	Lists all contents, including hidden files.
-b	Shows invisible characters in octal.
-c	Lists by creation/modification time.
-C	Lists in column (the default).
-d	Lists only the name of the directory, not the contents.
-f	Assumes that *names* are directories, not files.
-F	Flags executable filenames with an asterisk (*), directories with a slash (/), and symbolic links with @.
-g	Lists in long form, omitting the owner of the file.
-i	Lists the inode for each file.
-l	Lists the contents of a directory in long form.
-L	Lists the true files for symbolic links.
-m	Lists the contents across the screen, separated by commas.
-n	Same as **-l**, except uses numbers instead of names.
-o	Same as **-l**, except omits the group name.

Continued

-p	Displays a slash (/) at the end of every directory name.
-q	Lists contents with nonprinting characters represented by a question mark (?).
-r	Lists the contents in reverse order.
-R	Recursively lists subdirectories.
-s	Lists file sizes in blocks, instead of the default bytes.
-t	Lists the contents in order of time saved, beginning with the most recent.
-u	Lists files according to the most recent access time.
-x	Lists files in multicolumn format.

RELATED COMMANDS

chmod	Changes file-access permissions.
chgrp	Changes group.
chown	Changes file ownership.
find	Finds file.
ln	Links files.

mkdir   Make Directory

mkdir *options directories*

PURPOSE

Creates a new directory or directories.

EXAMPLE

`$ mkdir stuff`

(This creates a new directory called **stuff**.)

`$ mkdir -m 444 stuff`

(This creates a new directory called **stuff** and sets up file permissions of 444.)

OPTION

-m *mode*   Specifies the *mode* of the new directory.

more | Display File

more *options file(s)*

PURPOSE

Displays all or parts of a file one screenful at a time. Type **q** to quit; press **space bar** to continue.

EXAMPLE

```
$ more bigfile
```

(This displays a file named **bigfile**.)

OPTIONS

-c	Clears the screen before displaying the next page of the file. This can be quicker than watching pages scroll by.
-d	Displays a prompt at the bottom of the screen, involving brief instructions.
-f	Wraps text to fit the screen width and judge the page length accordingly.
-l	Ignores formfeeds (^L) at the end of a page.
-r	Displays control characters.
-s	Squeezes; ignores multiple blank lines.
-u	Ignore formatting characteristics like underlined text.
-w	Waits for user input before exiting.
-n	Sets window size by *n* lines.
+num	Starts output at line number *num.*

Continued

OPTIONS DURING FILE VIEWING

f	Goes to next full screen.
n	Displays next file.
p	Displays previous file.
q	Quits.

RELATED COMMAND

page	Displays file one page at a time.

mv   Move Files

mv *options sources target*

PURPOSE

Moves a file or multiple files into another directory or to
a new name in the current directory.

EXAMPLES

```
$ mv 1993.report /users/home/misc
```

(This moves the file **1993.report** to the directory named
/users/home/misc.)

```
$ mv 1993.report 1994.report
```

(This renames the file **1993.report** to the new filename
1994.report.)

```
$ mv 1993.report /users/home/misc/1994.report
```

(This saves the file **1993.report** under the name
1994.report in the directory **/users/home/misc**.)

```
$ mv -i 1993.report /users/home/misc/1994.report
mv: overwrite 1994.report?
```

(This saves the contents of the file **1993.report** to the new
name **1994.report** in the directory **/users/home/misc**.
The confirmation is required because **1994.report** already
exists.)

OPTIONS

-f   Moves file without checking for confirmation in case of an overwrite.

-i   Prompts users if action would overwrite an existing file.

RELATED COMMAND

cp   Copies files.

pack   Compress Files

pack *options file(s)*

PURPOSE

Compresses a file, decreasing its size by up to 50 percent. The original file is replaced by a new file, ending in **.z**. For instance, if you were to pack a file named **text**, the original file **text** is erased and a new **text.z** appears in the same directory.

Uncompress packed files with the **unpack** command.

OPTIONS

-	Display information about the compression.
-f	Packs the file even if no disk space is saved.

RELATED COMMANDS

compress	Compresses files.
pcat	Displays contents of packed files.
unpack	Unpacks contents of packed file.

page *options file(s)*

PURPOSE

Displays all or parts of a file. Type **q** to quit; press **space bar** to continue.

EXAMPLE

`$ page bigfile`

(This displays a file named **bigfile**.)

OPTIONS

-c	Clears the screen before displaying the next page of the file. This can be quicker than watching pages scroll by.
-d	Displays a prompt at the bottom of the screen, involving brief instructions.
-f	Wraps text to fit the screen width and judges the page length accordingly.
-l	Ignores formfeeds (^L) at the end of a page.
-r	Displays control characters.
-s	Squeezes; ignores multiple blank lines.
-u	Ignores formatting characteristics like underlined text.
-w	Waits for user input for exiting.
-*n*	Sets window size by *n* lines.
+*num*	Starts output at line number *num*.

Continued

OPTIONS DURING FILE VIEWING

f	Goes to next full screen.
n	Displays next file.
p	Displays previous file.
q	Quits.

RELATED COMMAND

more   Displays file one page at a time.

 Some UNIX variants use *pg* instead of *page*.

pcat — Display Packed Files

pcat *file(s)*

PURPOSE

Displays the contents of a packed file.

RELATED COMMANDS

pack   Compresses a file.

unpack   Uncompresses a file.

rm *options file(s)*

PURPOSE

Removes files, provided you're either the owner of the file or have write permission to the directory containing the file (though not necessarily to the file itself). If you don't have write permission to the file itself, you'll be prompted as to whether you really want to delete the file. This command can be used also to delete directories (remember that a directory is merely a file containing information about other files).

WARNING Use this command with caution. When a file is removed, it's really gone. Unless you have some undelete utilities at your disposal (for instance, there are versions of the *Norton Utilities* for some UNIX variants), you may want to be very careful with this command. We also use the *-i* option to verify our actions.

EXAMPLES

```
$ rm textfile
```

(This removes the file named **textfile**.)

```
$ rm textfile?
```

(This removes all files beginning with **textfile** and having a single extra character, like **textfile1**, **textfile2**, and so on.)

```
$ rm -r stuff
```

(This removes the directory named **stuff** and all its contents, including files and subdirectories.)

OPTIONS

-f   Removes files without verifying action with user.

-i   Removes files after verification from user.

-r   Recursively moves through subdirectories.

RELATED COMMAND

rmdir   Removes directory.

rmdir   Remove Directory

rmdir *options directory*

PURPOSE

Removes a directory. The directory must be empty. To empty a directory that contains other files and directories, use the **rm -r** command.

OPTIONS

-p   Removes the *directory* and any parent directory that is empty as a result of the action.

-s   Ignores error messages.

RELATED COMMAND

rm   Removes a file.

sdiff   Compares Files

sdiff *options file1 file2*

PURPOSE

Compares *file1* with *file2* and reports on the differences, as well as identical lines. Output occurs in four forms:

text text	Lines are identical.
text <	Line exists only in *file1*.
text >	Line exists only in *file2*.
*text	text*	Lines are different.

OPTIONS

-l   Reports only on lines that are identical in *file1*.

-o *outfile* Sends identical lines to *outfile*.

-s   Does not return identical lines.

-w*n*   Sets line length to *n*; default is 130.

RELATED COMMANDS

bdiff   Compares files.

cmp   Compares two files and tells you if the files are different.

diff   Compares files and reports *all* differing lines.

diff3   Compares three files.

File-Manipulation
Commands

split

Split Files

split *option file1 file2*

PURPOSE

Splits files into smaller files, based on line counts. The default is to create 1,000-line files. This command leaves the original *file1* intact. If *file2* is unnamed, the result files will be named **xaa**, **xab**, **xac**, and so on. If *file2* is named, **aa**, **ab**, **ac**, and so on will be appended to the end of the specified *file2* name.

If you're looking for more options when splitting a file—after all, using page lengths is a rather inflexible method of dividing files—use the more flexible **csplit** command covered elsewhere in this section.

EXAMPLE

```
$ split textfile newtext
```

(This would split **textfile** into smaller files. If **textfile** was 4,500 lines long, **split** would create five files—**newtextaa**, **newtextab**, **newtextac**, **newtextad**, and **newtextae**—with the first 4 files containing 1,000 lines, and the fifth containing 500 lines.)

OPTION

-*n*   Splits a file in *n*-line segments. (The default is 1,000 lines.)

RELATED COMMAND

csplit   Splits a file.

strings — Search File

strings *options file(s)*

PURPOSE

Looks for ASCII strings in binary files. Searches binary or object files for sequences of four or more printable characters, ending with newline or a null character. The **strings** command is useful for identifying binary files, such as object files or word-processor documents made by incompatible software.

OPTIONS

-a   Searches an entire file.

-n *n*   Sets minimum string length (the default is 4).

tail *options file*

PURPOSE

Displays the final 10 lines of a file.

OPTIONS

-f	"Follows" growth of file should changes be made while **tail** command is active. Use **Ctrl-D** to stop the process.
-r	Displays lines in reverse order. Not available on all systems.
-*n*b	Displays the last *n* blocks.
+*n*b	Displays all blocks after block *n*.
-*n*c	Displays the last *n* characters.
+*n*c	Displays all characters after n.
-*n*l	Displays the last *n* lines.
+*n*l	Displays all lines after line *n*.

RELATED COMMAND

head	Displays the first 10 lines of a file.

tar *options file(s)*

PURPOSE

Archives files to **tar** files, often on backup tapes. (In UNIX, a tape isn't always a tape—in this instance, it may be a tape, hard disk, or diskette.) Specified files can either replace existing files or be appended to existing files. **Tar** is also used to extract archived files from tape.

The usage for the **tar** command differs slightly from the rest of the UNIX command set. Options have two parts: a function option (each command must contain one of these), followed by other options. In addition, the hyphen (-) is not needed before options.

EXAMPLES

```
$ tar cvf /dev/mt0 /usr/users/kevin/memos
```

(This creates a new archive of all files in the directory **/usr/users/kevin/memos** on the device **/dev/mt0**; remember that devices in UNIX are treated as files.)

```
$ tar xvf /dev/mt0 `memo*`
```

(This extracts all files beginning with **memo** from the tape in **/dev/mt0**.)

FUNCTION OPTIONS

c	Creates a new **tar** archive.
r	Appends *files* to the end of the archive.
t	Prints out a table of contents.

163

u	Updates archive by appending *file(s)* if not on the tape or if modified.
x	Extracts files from within the **tar** archive.

OPTIONS

b*n*	Sets blocking factor to *n* (default is 1; maximum is 64).
f*dev*	Writes archive to *dev*; default is **/dev/mt0** on many systems.
l	Returns error messages about links that cannot be read.
L	Follows symbolic links.
m	Updates file-modification times to the time of extraction.
o	Changes ownership of extracted files to the current user. This is very useful if the archive was made by another user.
v	Verbose mode: prints out status information.
w	Waits for confirmation.

touch *options date file(s)*

PURPOSE

Changes a file's access time and modification time to the current date. If you try and change the date for a file that does not exist, **touch** will create a new file.

This value has more worth than meets the eye. For instance, some systems are set up to delete certain types of files that were created before a certain date and time; the **touch** command makes sure that the timestamp can be easily updated to avoid such deletions. In addition, some commands, such as **find** and **make**, use a file's timestamp at times.

Touch uses a *MMddhhmmyy* format for date and time:

MM	month (1–12)
dd	day (1–31)
hh	hour (00–23)
mm	minute (00–59)
yy	year (00–99)

OPTIONS

-a	Updates only the access time.
-c	Does not create a new file if none exists.
-m	Updates only the modification time.

RELATED COMMAND

date	Displays date and time.

uncompress   Uncompress File

uncompress *option file(s)*

PURPOSE

Uncompresses a compressed file, usually with a name ending in **.Z**.

OPTION

-c   Uncompresses without changing original *file(s)*.

RELATED COMMAND

compress   Compresses file.

unpack   Unpack File

unpack *file(s)*

PURPOSE

Unpacks a file shrunk with the **pack** commands. These
files usually end with **.z**.

RELATED COMMANDS

pack   Compresses a file.

pcat   Views a packed file.

Text-Processing Commands

These commands cover the various tools needed to edit and format text files.

awk *options 'pattern {action}'files*

PURPOSE

Actually a rudimentary programming language, **awk** is used mainly with text and database files—any structured file, really—and manipulates these files through editing, sorting, and searching.

    awk is an advanced tool that's far too complicated for this introductory work, as there's a whole set of specialized commands that are not even listed here, as you'll see from the short example. See the Bibliography for a list of UNIX tutorials that should cover **awk** in some form.

 awk **has been superseded somewhat by the** *nawk* (*new awk*) **command, which is also covered in this section. In** NOTE **addition, there's a version in GNU called** *gawk*.

EXAMPLE

```
$ awk '$1 ~ /Geisha/ {print $0}' workers
```

(This looks in the file **workers** for the string **Geisha** in the first column, which is designated by **$1**, and prints the entire record **$0** to the screen.)

OPTION

-F*sep*   Allows a field separator other than the default space or tab.

RELATED COMMAND

nawk   New version of **awk**.

col *options*

PURPOSE

Strips reverse backspaces and other control characters from a file formatted for multiple columns with a text editor like **tbl** or **nroff**. With these characters stripped, files can be displayed on older video screens as well as printed on printers that do not support reverse line-feeds.

This command is not usually used on its own, but rather as part of a longer command line with the eventual destination of a line printer. It is also handy when used with online manual pages, which are formatted.

EXAMPLE

```
$ cat kevin.report | col | lp
```

(This sends the file **kevin.report** to **col**, which stripped the formatting before printing with the **lp** command.)

OPTIONS

-b   Ignores backspace commands.

-f   Allows half linefeeds.

-p   Prints unknown escape characters as regular characters. (Don't use the option. It usually makes a mess of the final document.)

-x   Does not convert spaces to tabs.

Continued

RELATED COMMANDS

nroff	Text formatter.
tbl	Table editor.
troff	Text formatter.
vi	Text editor.

cut *options files*

PURPOSE

Displays a list of columns (specified with the **-c** option) or fields (specified with the **-f** option) from a file or a set of files. A column is exactly what the name describes—a row of characters with the same position on a line—while fields are separated by tabs. Both are referred to by numerals relative to the first column or field on the line.

EXAMPLES

```
$ cut -f1,3 workers > workers_phone
```

(This cuts fields 1 and 3 from the file **workers** and places them into a new file named **workers_phone**.)

```
$ cut -c1,3 workers > workers_phone
```

(This cuts columns 1 and 3 from the file **workers** and places them into a new file named **workers_phone**.)

OPTIONS

-c*list*   Used to cut columns specified by *list* from a file.

-d*character*   Substitutes *character* for the delimiter when the **-f** option is used. If a nonalphabetic character is to be used as the delimiter (such as a space), it must be enclosed in single quote marks.

Continued

-f*list*   Used to cut field specified by *list* from a file.

-s   Suppresses (does not return) lines lacking a delimiter; used with the **-f** option.

RELATED COMMANDS

grep   Finds text in files.

join   Joins lines found in multiple files.

paste   Joins two files in vertical columns.

deroff *options files*

PURPOSE

Removes formatting commands inserted by the **tbl**, **eqm**, **mm**, **nroff**, and **troff** formatting commands.

EXAMPLES

```
$ deroff kevin.report
```

(This removes all formatting commands from the file **kevin.report**.)

```
$ deroff -mm workers
```

(This removes requests from **mm**-formatted files.)

OPTIONS

-ml	Deletes lists from **mm**-formatted files.
-mm	Strips formatting from **mm**-formatted files.
-ms	Strips formatting from **ms**-formatted files.

RELATED COMMANDS

col	Strips control characters.
eqn	Equation editor.
nroff	Text formatter.
tbl	Table editor.
troff	Text formatter.

ed   Editor

ed *options file*

PURPOSE

A rudimentary text editor, superseded by more sophisti-
cated tools like **vi** or **ex**. **Ed** works in two modes—input
and command—with very little feedback. It is still used
by UNIX in nondirect ways; for instance, the **diff**
command calls on the **ed** command.

OPTIONS

-C   Allows for the editing of encrypted files.
                  (This option can be used only in the United
                  States, due to export regulations.)

-p *string*   Substitutes *string* for the standard
                  command prompt (the **ed** default is *).

-s   Suppresses information about files sizes,
                  diagnostic information, and the **!** prompt
                  for shell commands.

-x   Allows for the editing of encrypted files.
                  (This option can be used only in the United
                  States, due to export regulations.)

RELATED COMMANDS

crypt   Encrypts files.
vi   Text editor.

eqn — Equation Formatter

eqn *options files*

PURPOSE

Formats equations created by **troff**, for eventual printing by a printer or typesetting machines. **Eqn** commands are placed into a **troff** file, and then the file is run through **eqn**, with the output usually piped to **troff** and then piped to a printer. If you are using **nroff** as a text processor, use the **neqn** command.

MACROS

These macros are to be used within the *troff*-**created files, not on an** *eqn* **command line.**

.EQ	Starts typesetting mathematical characters.
.EN	Stops typesetting mathematical characters.

OPTIONS

-f*font*	Uses font *font*.
-p*n*	Reduces size of superscripts and subscripts by *n* points.
-s*n*	Reduces size of all text by *n* points.
-T*dev*	Formats for the typesetting *dev*, as defined in the TYPESETTER= environment variable.

Continued

RELATED COMMANDS

neqn	Equation preprocessor used with **nroff**.
nroff	Text formatter.
tbl	Table editor.
troff	Text formatter.
vi	Text editor.

fmt *options files*

PURPOSE

Formats texts in a limited fashion—usually to justify text to the right margin only. Text editors like **vi** don't automatically perform this task, so this command is frequently invoked within the **vi** (**emacs**, on the other hand, formats text through the **Esc-Q** command). In addition, the output of this command is usually piped to a printer command. **Fmt** is not available on all systems.

OPTIONS

-c	Does not format the first two lines.
-*n*	Limits the size of lines to *n* columns wide, instead of the default 72.
-s	Splits long lines but ignores short lines.
-w*n*	Limits the size of lines to *n* columns wide, instead of the default 72. (This option is not supported in BSD.)

fold *options files*

PURPOSE

Formats text to a specific width, even if the break occurs in the middle of a word.

OPTIONS

-n   Limits the size of lines to *n* columns wide, instead of the default 80.

-w*n*   Limits the size of lines to *n* columns wide, instead of the default 80. (This option is not supported in BSD.)

PURPOSE

Actually a rudimentary programming language, **nawk** is used mainly with text and database files—any structured file, really—and manipulates these files through editing, sorting, and searching.

    nawk is an advanced tool that's far too complicated for this introductory work, as there's a whole set of specialized commands that are not even listed here. See the Bibliography for a list of UNIX tutorials that should cover **nawk** in some form.

nawk **has superseded the** *awk* **command, which is also covered in this section. In addition, there's a version in** N O T E **GNU called** *gawk*.

neqn *options files*

PURPOSE

Formats equations created by **nroff**, for eventual printing by a printer or typesetting machines. **Neqn** commands are placed into a **nroff** file, and then the file is run through **neqn**, with the output piped to a printer. If you are using **troff** as a text processor, use the **eqn** command.

MACROS

NOTE

These are to be used within the *nroff*-**created files, not on an** *neqn* **command line.**

.EQ   Starts typesetting mathematical characters.

.EN   Stops typesetting mathematical characters.

OPTIONS

-f*font*   Uses font *font*.

-p*n*   Reduces size of superscripts and subscripts by *n* points.

-s*n*   Reduces size of all text by *n* points.

-T*dev*   Formats for the typesetting *dev*, as defined in the TYPESETTER= environment variable.

Continued

RELATED COMMANDS

eqn   Equation preprocessor used with **nroff**.

nroff   Text formatter.

tbl   Table editor.

troff   Text formatter.

vi   Text editor.

newform   Format Text

newform *options file(s)*

PURPOSE

Formats text files by adding and removing characters, changing tab settings, and so on. The **newform** command should be viewed as a down-and-dirty text formatter for those who know precisely what they want; since there's little interactivity between the user and the command, it's easy to make unwanted changes.

OPTIONS

-a*n*	Appends *n* characters to the end of each line.
-b*n*	Removes *n* characters from the beginning of each line.
-c*char*	Uses *char* instead of the default space with the **-a** and **-p** options. (The **-c** option must appear before **-a** or **-p** on the command line.)
-e*n*	Removes *n* characters from the end of each line.
-i*tabspec*	Sets the tab format defined by *tabspec*. (See the **tabs** command for more information.)
-l*n*	Sets the default line length in *n* characters; the default is 72.
-o*tabspec*	Converts tabs to spaces, as defined by *tabspec*. (See the **tabs** command for more information.)
-p*n*	Adds *n* characters to the beginning of each line.
-s	Removes characters before the first tab and places them at the end of the line.

nl *options file*

PURPOSE

Inserts line numbers at the beginning of every line of the file and breaks the file into logical page segments, with the first line of each page numbered *1*.

EXAMPLE

```
$ nl -ba -ht -ft textfile
```

(This formats every line in the file **textfile**, including headers and footers.)

OPTIONS

-b*type*	Numbers lines according to one of four *type*s:
	a All lines.
	n No lines.
	p*str* Lines containing *str*.
	t Only lines containing text.
-d*xy*	Changes *xy* as the delimiter for logical page sections.
-f*type*	Numbers the footers; see the **-b** option for *type*s.
-h*type*	Numbers the headers; see the **-b** option for *type*s.
-i*n*	Increases numbers by *n* increments (default is 1).
-l*n*	Compresses *n* of blank lines to one line.

Continued

-n*format*	Inserts line numbers in one of three *formats*:
	ln Left justify, no zeroes.
	rn Right justify, no zeroes.
	rz Right justify.
-p	Does not reset numbering at the beginning of every page.
-s*char*	Inserts *char* between line numbers and text (default is tab).
-v*n*	Starts page numbering at *n* (default is 1).
-w*n*	Shows line numbers in *n* columns (default is 6).

nroff *options file(s)*

PURPOSE

Formats text for printing on a daisywheel or dot-matrix printer. (The related command of **troff** prepares files for printing on a laser printer or a typesetter.) The **nroff** command interprets commands already inserted into a text file. For instance, to flush all lines right, you would insert the **.ad r** command within a text file. (This is known as a *dot command*, since it begins with a dot.) When you run the **nroff** command, **nroff** will find the **.ad r** command within the text and format the text accordingly.

The majority of information associated with **nroff** has to do with these commands inserted within files in anticipation of output by **nroff**. For the most part, the same dot commands are used by **troff** and **nroff**, although there's a set of additional commands special to **troff**.

A ton of formatting options are available with **troff** and **nroff**—84 formatting requests alone, plus many registers and characters. We suggest that you check your system documentation should you want more information about these commands. Another useful action would be to check out works specifically on **troff** and **nroff**, which are listed in the Bibliography.

EXAMPLES

```
$ nroff textfile | lp
```

(This formats the file **textfile** with **nroff** and sends the results to the line printer.)

Continued

```
$ nroff textfile | more
```

(This formats the file **textfile** and prints the results on the screen one page at a time.)

RELATED COMMAND

troff   Text formatter.

paste *options file(s)*

PURPOSE

them

Merges files and places then side by side. For instance, the first line of *file1* will be followed by the first line of *file2* in a second column; a tab separates the two columns.

OPTIONS

-           Uses standard input as input (handy when piping output to the command).

-d'*char*' Use *char* as the delimiter between columns, instead of the default tab. *Char* can be any character, or one of the following:
            \n   Newline.
            \t   Tab.
            ****   Backslash.

RELATED COMMANDS

cut   Cuts fields.
join   Joins files.

sort   Sorts Files

sort *options files*

PURPOSE

Sorts the lines of named *files*, usually in alphabetical order. Commands like **comm** and **join** require sorted files in order to work.

OPTIONS

-b	Ignores leading spaces and tabs.
-c	Checks if *files* are already sorted. If they are, **sort** does nothing.
-d	Sorts in dictionary order (ignores punctuation).
-f	Ignores case.
-i	Ignores non-ASCII characters.
-m	Merges files that have already been sorted.
-M	Sorts the files assuming the first three characters are months.
-n	Sorts in numeric order.
-o*file*	Stores output in *file*. The default is to send output to standard output.
-r	Reverses sort.
-t*c*	Separates fields with character (default is tab).
-u	Unique output: If merge creates identical lines, uses only the first.
-y*k*	Sets aside *k* kilobytes of memory for the sort. If *k* is not specified, the maximum

Continued

possible will be allocated.

-z*n*   Provides a maximum of *n* characters per
              line of input.

+*n***[-***m***]**   Skips *n* fields before sorting and then sorts
              through line *m*.

spell — Check Spelling

spell *options files*

PURPOSE

Returns incorrectly spelled words in a file. You can also use **spell** to compare spellings against a sorted word file of your own creation. Since it returns only "incorrect" spellings—that is, words not contained in a file of correctly spelled words—**spell** is not as useful as you might think.

EXAMPLE

```
$ spell textfile
```

(This checks the spellings in the file **textfile**.)

```
$ spell +morewords textfile
```

(This checks the spellings in the file **textfile**, both against the main file and the user-created file, **morewords**.)

OPTIONS

-b	Checks for spelling based on British usage.
-l	Checks all included files associated with the target file.
-x	Shows every possible stem of target words.
+*filename*	Creates a sorted file (*filename*) of correctly spelled words.

tabs *tabspec options*

PURPOSE

Sets the tab settings. The default settings are every eighth column (1, 9, 17, and so on). This command supports several preconfigured tab settings for specific languages (see the Options list), or you can set the tabs manually.

TABSPECS

-8	Sets tabs every eighth column (1, 9, 17, and so on). Default.
-a	IBM S/370 assembler (1, 10, 16, 36, 72).
-a2	IBM S/370 assembler (1, 10, 16, 40, 72).
-c	COBOL (1, 8, 12, 16, 20, 55).
-c2	Compact COBOL (1, 6, 10, 14, 49).
-c3	Expanded COBOL (1, 6, 10, 14, 18, 22, 26, 30, 34, 38, 42, 46, 50, 54, 58, 62, 67).
-f	FORTRAN (1, 7, 11, 15, 19, 23).
-p	PL/1 (1, 5, 9, 13, 17, 21, 25, 29, 33, 37, 41, 45, 49, 53, 57, 61).
-s	SNOBOL (1, 10, 55).
-u	UNIVAC 1100 Assembler (1, 12, 20, 44).

OPTIONS

+mn	Sets left margin to n (default is 10).
-T*type*	Sets terminal *type* (default is TERM).

tbl *file*

PURPOSE

This preprocessor to **nroff** or **troff** formats tables for eventual printing. In this day of WYSIWYG, a tool like **tbl** may seem positively archaic, but it still is a useful tool. With **tbl**, you insert formatting commands within the text file. When you run **tbl** on a command line and then pipe the output to **nroff** or **troff**, the formatting commands are interpreted, and you end up with a file ready for either printing or viewing on the screen.

These formatting commands are rather complicated for the uninitiated. Be warned that it may take quite a bit of effort on the part of the beginner to end up with acceptable output from **tbl**.

EXAMPLES

```
$ tbl textfile | troff |lp
```

(This formats the file **textfile**, first with **tbl** and then with **troff**, and sends the subsequent formatted file to the line printer.)

```
.TS
center, box, tab(%);
cb s s.
Big Ten Standings

—
.T&
1| 1 | 1;
Minnesota%5%1
```

Continued

```
Michigan%2%3
Wisconsin%1%4
.TE
```

(This rather rudimentary table would show three columns—headed by Minnesota, Michigan, and Wisconsin—with a bold banner, **Big Ten Standings**.)

FORMATTING OPTIONS

NOTE **These are only a few of the major formatting options. Check your documentation or your online manual pages for more information.**

.TS Table Start. This option *must* begin the area formatted by **tbl**.

allbox Boxes the table and every entry within the table.

box Boxes the table.

center Centers the table.

; Ends the layout for the table.

c Center.

l Flush left.

r Flush right.

a Aligns alphabetic entries.

n Aligns numerical entries.

Continued

b	Bold.
i	Italics.
f*fontname*	Font *fontname*.
p*n*	Point size in *n*.
v*n*	Vertical line spacing, *n* points.
.TE	Table End. This option *must* end the area formatting by **tbl**.

Translate Characters

tr *options string1 string2*

PURPOSE

Translates characters as part of a global search-and-replace procedure. **Tr** is a quirky command in its syntax, as you'll see in the Examples.

EXAMPLES

```
$ tr '<TAB>' , < textfile
```

(This changes every tab in the file **textfile** to a comma. Note the strange notation for input.)

```
$ cat textfile | tr '[A-Z]' '[a-z]' > newfile
```

(This takes input from **textfile**, changes every uppercase letter to its lowercase equivalent, and then saves the output to **newtextfile**.)

OPTIONS

-c	Uses all characters *not* covered by *string1*.
-d	Deletes the characters covered in *string1*.
-s	Squeezes repeated use of a character into a single use.

troff *options file(s)*

PURPOSE

Formats text for printing on a laser printer or a typesetter. (The related command of **nroff** prepares files for printing on a daisywheel or dot-matrix printer.) The **troff** command interprets commands already inserted into a text file. For instance, to flush all lines right, you would insert the **.ad r** command within a text file. (This is known as a *dot command*, since it begins with a dot.) When you run the **troff** command, **troff** will find the **.ad r** command within the text and format the text accordingly.

The majority of information associated with **troff** has to do with these commands inserted within files in anticipation of output by **troff**. For the most part, the same dot commands are used by **troff** and **nroff**, although there's a set of additional files special to **troff**.

A ton of formatting options are available with **troff** and **nroff**—84 formatting requests alone, plus many registers and characters. We suggest that you check your system documentation should you want more information about these commands. Another useful action would be to check out works specifically on **troff** and **nroff**, which are listed in the Bibliography.

EXAMPLES

```
$ troff textfile | lp
```

(This formats the file **textfile** with **troff** and sends the results to the line printer, which **must** be a laser printer or typesetting machine.)

Continued

```
$ troff textfile | more
```

(This formats the file **textfile** and prints the results on the screen one page at a time.)

RELATED COMMANDS

eqn	Equation formatter.
nroff	Text formatter.
tbl	Table formatter.

uniq   Find Unique Lines

uniq *options file1 file2*

PURPOSE

Identifies and removes duplicate lines from a sorted file. (Use the **sort** command to sort the file.)

EXAMPLES

```
$ uniq textfile
```

(This removes all duplicate lines in the file **textfile**.)

```
$ uniq textfile text.uniq
```

(This removes all duplicate lines in the file **textfile** and saves them to **text.uniq**.)

OPTIONS

-c	Counts; precedes lines by the number of times they appear.
-d	Deletes all duplicate lines, except the first.
-u	Unique—prints only lines that appear once.
-*n*	Skips the first *n* lines in a field.
+*n*	Skips the first *n* characters in a field.

RELATED COMMAND

sort	Sorts a file.

vi *options file(s)*

PURPOSE

A full-screen text editor, with many useful options. This summary lists the options, but not all the editing commands possible when editing a file. For a list of these commands—and there are indeed *many* of them—either run the **man** command for **vi** or else check out a book that contains a reference section on **vi** commands.

The **vi** editor runs mainly in two modes: command mode and insert mode. In insert mode, you enter text. In command mode, you modify text or issue commands. (We list some of the more useful commands here, but many more are available.) Press **Escape** to exit input mode and return to command mode.

For more information on **vi,** we suggest that you pick up a more complete UNIX tutorial, such as *Teach Yourself UNIX* (MIS:Press, 1992). While **vi** isn't exactly the most complex command possible, it does require a little background and a little explanation of the underlying concepts. We list some of the more useful commands here, but many more are available.

EXAMPLES

```
$ vi
```

(This begins a **vi** text-editing session.)

```
$ vi textfile
```

(This starts **vi** with the file **textfile** loaded for editing.)

OPTIONS

-c *command*	Starts **vi** and runs *command*.
-C	Edits an encrypted file (see the **crypt** command for more information).
-l	Runs **vi** in LISP mode for editing LISP files.
-L	Lists the files that were saved despite a system failure.
-r *file*	Recovers *file* after a system crash.
-R	Runs in read-only mode, which means that files cannot be changed.
-w *n*	Sets window size to *n* lines of text.
-x	Creates an encrypted file (see the **crypt** command for more information).
+	Starts **vi** on the last line of the file.
+ *line*	Starts **vi** with *line* as the top line in the window.

VI COMMANDS

/ *pattern*	Searches for *pattern*, going forward.
/ *pattern*	Searches for *pattern*, going backward.
n **G**	Goes to line number *n*.
h	Same as the left arrow key. Useful for keyboards lacking arrow keys.
j	Same as the down arrow key. Useful for keyboards lacking arrow keys.
k	Same as the up arrow key. Useful for keyboards lacking arrow keys.

Continued

l	Same as the right arrow key. Useful for keyboards lacking arrow keys.
Ctrl-F	Goes forward one page.
Ctrl-B	Goes backward one page.
ZZ	Saves file and exits.
:w	Saves file.
:q	Quits without saving file.
:wq	Saves file and quits the command.
:n	Goes to next file on the command line.
:n!	Goes to next file on the command line, even if you haven't saved the current file.
:q!	Quits without saving file.
dw	Deletes word.
dd	Deletes line.
i	Enters insert mode.
a	Enters append mode, inserting after current position.

RELATED COMMANDS

crypt	Encrypts files.
nroff	Text formatter.
tbl	Table editor.
troff	Text formatter.

wc *options file(s)*

PURPOSE

Counts the number of words, characters, and lines in a text file or files. The terse output presents the number of lines, followed by the words and characters.

OPTIONS

-c	Prints only the number of characters.
-l	Prints only the number of lines.
b	Prints only the number of words.

Printing Commands

These commands cover the actual printing commands as well the commands that prepare files for printing.

PURPOSE

Displays up to 10 characters in large letters using asterisks (*) or number signs (#), depending on your system.

EXAMPLE

```
$ banner kevin
```

creates the following output:

```
#     #  ######  #     #   #   #      #
#  #   #  #        #     #   #   ##     #
###    ####     #     #   #   # #    #
# #    #        #     #   #   #  #   #
#  #   #         #  #    #   #    ###
#     #  ######    ##     #   #      #
```

cancel *options printer*

PURPOSE

Cancels pending printer jobs initiated with the **lp** command. You can either specify the job ID or printer to be canceled. (Privileged users can use the command to cancel jobs created by a specific user.)

OPTIONS

job-id   Cancels the specific *job-id*.

-u *user*   Cancels the print requests made by a specific *user*.

Printing
Commands

lp *options files*

PURPOSE

Sends a print request to a printer. Can be used to print
multiple files with one request. On some systems, you
may need to use the **lpr** command instead. Not all of
these options are available on every system, due to configuration differences. Check with your system administrator to see what options are supported.

OPTIONS

-c	Copies the file to a print spooler before sending the request.
-d *printer*	Specifies a printer other than the default printer.
-d any	Used with the **-f** and **-s** options, to find any printer that support a form or character set specified by *name*.
-f *name*	Prints on the form *name*; used in conjunction with the **-d any** option.
-H *action*	Prints according to one of these actions:

	hold	Suspends current or pending print job.
	immediate	Prints immediately after current job is completed.
	resume	Resumes suspended print job.

-m	Sends a mail message to the user when the file is printed.
-n *num*	Prints *num* number of copies (the default is 1).

-o *option*	Sets printer-specific options:	
	cpi=*n*	Print *n* characters per inch; **pica**, **elite**, or **compressed** can be used instead of *n*.
	length=*n*	Page length, specified in inches (*n*i), lines (*n*), or centimeters (*n*c).
	lpi=*n*	Prints *n* lines per inch.
	nobanner	Does not print the banner page.
	nofilebreak	Does not print form feed between files.
	stty=*list*	Returns a *list* of options for **stty**.
	width=*n*	Page width, specified in inches (*n*i), lines (*n*), or centimeters (*n*c).
-P *list*	Prints the page numbers specified by *list*.	
-q *level*	Sets a priority *level* for the print job (lowest is 39).	
-s	Suppresses messages from **lp**.	
-S *name*	Uses the character set or printwheel *name*.	
-t *title*	Prints *title* banner on every page.	
-T *type*	Prints on a printer that supports *type*. (See your system administrator about what *type*s are supported.)	
-w	Sends a terminal message to the user when the file is printed.	
-y *list*	Prints according to locally defined nodes, contained in *list*.	

Continued

RELATED COMMANDS

cancel	Cancels print requests.
lpsched	Turns on the print spooler.
lpshut	Turns off the print spooler.
lpstat	Shows printer status.

lpsched

PURPOSE

Turns on a print spooler. A print spooler stores print requests in memory, allocating them to printers. This allows several print requests to be stored in RAM simultaneously, freeing the users who originate the print requests to go on with their work. This command can be run from a prompt but is more effectively used when placed in the **rc** file, where it will be launched when the system starts. Normally, system adminstrators run **lpsched**.

OPTIONS

None.

RELATED COMMAND

lpshut　　　Turns off the print spooler.

lpshut   Stop Print Spooler

lpsched

PURPOSE

Turns off a print spooler.

OPTIONS

None.

RELATED COMMAND

lpsched   Turns on the print spooler.

lpstat   Show Printer Status

lpstat *options*

PURPOSE

Returns the status of print requests, either individually or systemwide.

OPTIONS

-a [*list*]	Tells whether the *list* of printers or class names is accepting print requests.
-c [*list*]	Displays the names of all class names and printers contained in *list*.
-d	Shows the name of the default destination printer.
-D	Shows a description of the printer when used with **-p**.
-f [*list*]	Displays the forms supported by the system in *list*. The **-l** option returns a description of these forms.
-o [*list*]	Returns the status of output requests by printer name, class name, and request ID.
-p [*list*]	Shows the status of all printers in *list*.
-r	Shows whether the print scheduler (or print spooler, as controlled by **lpsched**) is on or off.
-R	Shows the position of a job in the queue.
-s	Summarizes print status.
-S [*list*]	Displays character sets or printwheel supported in *list*.
-t	Shows all status information.

Continued

-u [*list*]	Shows the status of requests made by users on *list*. In this instance, *list* refers to:

user	*User* on the local machine.
all	All users.
host **!** *user*	*User* on machine *host*.
host **!all**	All users on *host*.
all! *user*	*User* not on local machine.
all!all	All users.

-v [*list*]	Displays pathnames of devices for all printers (or printers listed in *list*.)

RELATED COMMANDS

cancel	Cancels print requests.
lp	Prints files.
lpsched	Turns on the print spooler.

pr *options file(s)*

PURPOSE

Prepares a file for printing to standard output. If you want to print to the default printer, for instance, you pipe the output to **lp**. Each printed page contains a header, which includes a page number, filename, date, and time. There are many options for formatting the file, such as multiple columns.

EXAMPLES

```
$ pr textfile | lp
```

(This prepares the file **textfile** for printing and then sends the result to the default line printer.)

```
$ pr textfile
```

(This prepares the file **textfile** for printing and displays the results on the screen.)

OPTIONS

-a	Prints multiple columns in rows across the page.
-d	Double-spaces the text.
-ec*n*	Sets tabs (as specified by *c*) to every *n*th position (default is 8).
-f	Separate pages by form feeds, not blank lines.
-F	Folds input lines to avoid truncation.

Continued

-h *text*	Prints the header *text* at the beginning of the output.
-i*cn*	Replaces white space with *c* (default is tab) every *n*th position (default is 8).
-l*n*	Sets the page length to *n* (default is 66).
-m	Merges input files, placing each in its own column.
-n*cn*	Numbers lines with numbers *n* digits in length (default is 5), separated from the text by *c* (default is a tab).
-o*n*	Offsets each line by *n* spaces.
-p	Pauses between pages; handy when reading off of a screen.
-r	Suppresses messages about files that can't be found.
-s*c*	Separates columns with *c* (default is tab).
-t	Does not print page header.
-w*c*	Sets the page width to *n* (default is 72).
+*num*	Begins printing at page *num*.
-*num*	Prints output with *num* columns.

RELATED COMMANDS

cat	Concatenates files.
join	Joins files.
paste	Concatenates files horizontally.

Communications Commands

These commands allow you to communicate with other users (both on your own system as well as on other systems) and systems.

ct *options -speed -w -x system*

PURPOSE

Allows you to call another terminal and log on a remote UNIX system via modem or direct line.

EXAMPLES

```
$ ct -s9600 5555555
```

(This calls the telephone number 555-5555 at 9600 bps.)

```
$ ct -s9600 nicollet
```

(This calls the remote system **nicollet** at 9600 bps, so long as **nicollet** appears on a list of system supported by the **uuname** command.)

OPTIONS

-h	Prevents hang-ups.
-v	Outputs status to standard output.
-s*bps*	Sets bits-per-second rate.
-w*min*	Waits *min* minutes for remote system to answer.
-x*n*	Debugging mode at *n* level.
system	Phone number or system name.

RELATED COMMANDS

cu	Calls up another system.
uuname	Lists UNIX-to-UNIX system names.

cu *options system*

PURPOSE

Calls up another UNIX system or terminal, or non-UNIX bulletin-board service or online services, via modem or direct line. Other computer systems have a separate telecommunications package. In UNIX, telecommunications capabilities are built into the operating system.

EXAMPLES

```
$ cu -s9600 5555555
```

(This calls the telephone number 555-5555 at 9600 bps.)

```
$ cu -s9600 nicollet
```

(This calls the remote system **nicollet** at 9600 bps, so long as **nicollet** appears on a list of system supported by the **uuname** command.)

Communication Commands

OPTIONS

-b*n*	Sets bit length to 7 or 8.
-c*name*	Searches the **UUCP Device** file for *name*.
-d	Sets diagnostics mode.
-e	Sets even parity. (Opposite of **-o**.)
-h	Sets half-duplex.
-l*port*	Specifies specific port for communications.
-n	Prompts the user for a telephone number.
-o	Sets odd parity. (Opposite of **-e**.)

Continued

-srate   Sets bits-per-second rate (300, 1200, 2400, 9600, etc.).

-t   Calls an ASCII terminal.

ONLINE COMMANDS

NOTE

These commands are to be run after a connection to the remote system.

~!command   Runs *command* on the local system.

~$command   Runs *command* on the local system and then send the output to the remote system.

~%cd *directory* Changes to directory *directory* on the local system.

~%put *file*   Copies *file* from the local system to the remote system.

~$take *file*   Takes *file* from the remote system and places it on the local system.

~!   Exits **cu**.

~.   Disconnects the telephone link between the two systems.

~?   Displays a listing of all online commands.

RELATED COMMANDS

ct   Calls terminal.

uuname   Lists UNIX-to-UNIX system names.

ftp — File Transfer Protocol

This command is covered in its own section. See Section 8, "FTP Commands," for more details.

logname

PURPOSE

Returns your login name—or more precisely, the value of the **$LOGNAME** environment variable.

OPTIONS

None.

RELATED COMMAND

login   Login a system.

mailx *options users*

PURPOSE

Used to send and receive mail to other users. This command supersedes the **mail** command found in many older versions of UNIX. Files can be attached to **mailx**-created messages. See the **uuencode** command for more information.

Some system administrators also install other mail front ends in their systems, such as **elm**, **mailtool**, or **dtmail**. Check with your system administrator to see if you should be using **mailx** or another mail program.

EXAMPLES

```
$ mailx erc
Subject:
```

(This sends a mail message to **erc**. After the **mailx** command is given, the system then prompts for a subject and a message text. After you're finished editing text, press **Ctrl-D** to end the input.)

```
$ mailx erc < memo
```

(This sends the contents of the file **memo** to **erc** in the form of a mail message.)

OPTIONS

-d	Sets debugging mode.
-e	Checks for mail, without printing it.
-f *file*	Stores mail in file named *file* (default is **mbox**).

Continued

-F	Stores mail in file named after the first recipient of the message.
-h *n*	Sets number of network hops to *n*.
-i	Ignores interrupts.
-I	Saves newsgroup and article IDs; used in conjunction with **-f**.
-n	Ignores startup **mailx.rc** file.
-N	Ignores mail headers.
-r *address*	Specifies a return *address* for your mail.
-s *subject*	Enters *subject* in the "Subject:" field, avoiding the prompt.
-T *file*	Records message and article IDs in *file*.
-U	Converts a **uucp** address to an Internet address.
-V	Version number.

RELATED COMMANDS

uucp	UNIX-to-UNIX copy.
uuencode	Encodes files for transmission with **mailx**.

mesg   Enable/Disable Messages

mesg *options*

PURPOSE

Grants or denies permission to other users to send you messages via the **write** or **talk** commands.

EXAMPLES

$ mesg -y

(This allows messages.)

$ mesg -n

(This forbids messages.)

OPTIONS

-n   Forbids messages.

-y   Allows messages.

RELATED COMMANDS

talk   Talks with another user via the network.

write   Sends a message to a user.

notify   Notify of Mail

notify *options*

PURPOSE

Notifies a user when new mail arrives. This command is not available on all systems. Some systems have a **checkmail** command instead.

OPTIONS

-m *file*	Saves mail messages to *file*, when the **-y** option is enabled.
-n	Disables mail notification.
-y	Enables mail notification.

RELATED COMMAND

mailx	Sends and reads mail.

rcp *options source target*

PURPOSE

Copies files to and from remote systems. This command assumes that you have permissions in the target directory. Generally, this command is used in conjunction with the **rlogin** command: First you log on a remote machine with **rlogin** and then transfer files with the **rcp** command. To name remote files, use *hostname:filename.*

EXAMPLES

```
$ rcp nicollet:/u/erc/report.1994 report.copy
```

(This copies **nicollet:/u/erc/report.1994** on remote machine **nicollet** to **report.copy** on the local machine.)

```
$ rcp report.1993 attila:/users/kevin
```

(This copies local file **attila:/users/kevin** to the **/users/kevin** directory on remote machine **attila**.)

OPTIONS

-p	Preserves the permissions of the source file.
-r	Recursively copies each subdirectory.

Continued

RELATED COMMANDS

ftp	File-transfer protocol.
mailx	Sends and receives mail.
rlogin	Remote login.
uucp	UNIX-to-UNIX copy.

rlogin *options hostname*

PURPOSE

Logs in to a remote system. A list of the available *host-names* is stored in the **/etc/hosts/.rhosts** file. If your *local* hostname is listed in the **.rhosts** file in your home directory on the *remote* machine, then you won't need to enter a password. Your local computing session is suspended when you're logged on a remote machine. Any UNIX commands you use will be run on the remote machine. When you're finished on the remote system, use an **exit** command or press **Ctrl-D** to end the connection.

OPTIONS

-8	Uses 8-bit data (default is 7 bits).
-e *c*	Uses c as the default escape character (default is ~).
-l *username*	Remotely logs in under the new *username*, instead of the name on your local host.

RELATED COMMANDS

ftp	File-transfer protocol.
mailx	Sends and receives mail.
rcp	Remote copy.
uucp	UNIX-to-UNIX copy.

rsh   Remote Shell

rsh *options hostname command*

PURPOSE

Starts a remote shell on a remote machine, executing a command on the remote machine. On some systems, **rsh** refers to the *restricted* shell. The remote shell then is called **remsh**.

OPTIONS

-l *user*   Logs in *user* to the remote machine.

-n   Diverts input to **/dev/null**, which can be useful when troubleshooting.

sum *option filename(s)*

PURPOSE

Computes and prints a checksum and block count for a specified *file*. While this command isn't specifically geared toward communications, it's used most often when communicating files back and forth to remote systems, ensuring that the transferred files are the same size on both ends.

The BSD version of this command differs slightly. To match the results of a BSD-generated **sum** command, use the **-r** option.

OPTION

-r   Uses alternative algorithm to compute checksum and size; matches BSD version of command.

RELATED COMMAND

wc   Word count.

talk   Talk to Other User

talk *username[@hostname] terminal*

PURPOSE

Carries on a conversation with another user on the network. The command splits your screen into two areas: The top half contains your typing, while the bottom contains messages from the other user. The **write** command is similar, except that **write** is geared for single messages and not for an ongoing dialog. Press **Ctrl-D** to exit.

OPTIONS

user	Other *user*, obviously.
hostname	The *hostname* of the machine the *user* is logged on, if the user isn't logged in to your local machine.
terminal	Specified a *tty* should the *user* be logged on more than one terminal.

RELATED COMMANDS

mesg	Blocks communications.
write	Writes a message to another terminal.

telnet *system port*

PURPOSE

Logs in to a remote system using the TELNET protocol. After you login the remote system, your prompt will change to the **telnet** prompt (`telnet>`), from which you can enter TELNET commands. **Telnet** also supports an input mode, where you can enter commands directly on the remote system. Use the escape character (**Ctrl-]** or **^**, depending on your system setup) to switch between the two modes.

OPTIONS

system   Name of remote system or its network address.

port   Optional port identification.

ONLINE COMMANDS

close   Ends remote session and exits the program.

display *values* Displays **set** and **toggle** values.

mode *mode*   Changes mode to **character** or **line**.

open *system*   Opens connection to *system*.

quit   Ends remote session and exits the program.

send *chars*   Sends special characters to the remote system:

      ao   Aborts output.

      ayt   Are you there?

Continued

brk	Break.
ec	Erase character.
el	Erase line.
escape	Escape.
ga	Go ahead.
ip	Interrupt process.
nop	No operation.
synch	Synch.
?	Help for **send** command.

set *value*   Sets one of the following values:

echo	Local echo on or off.
eof	End of file.
erase	Erase character.
escape	New Escape character.
flushoutput	Flush output.
interrupt	Interrupts process.
kill	Erase line.
quit	Break.

status   Displays status.

toggle *values*   Changes one of the following values:

autoflush	Send **interrupt** or **quit** to remote system.
autosynch	Synch after **interrupt** or **quit**.
crmod	Convert **CR** to **CR LF**.
debug	Debugging mode.

Continued

	localchars	Convert local commands to remote control.
	netdata	Convert hexadecimal display of network data.
	options	Protocol processing.
	?	Display settings.
z	Suspends **telnet**.	
?	Displays summary of online commands.	

RELATED COMMAND

rlogin   Remote login.

uucp *options source! destination! file(s)*

PURPOSE

Copies files to and from remote UNIX system. The *file(s)* may also be entire directories. Normally the destination is a public, secure directory named **uucppublic**, to prevent unwanted visitors from roaming around a UNIX system.

EXAMPLE

    $ uucp textfile harmar!/usr/users/geisha/uucppublic

(This copies the file **textfile** to the machine named **harmar** in the directory **/usr/users/geisha/uucpublic**.)

OPTIONS

-c	Copies the actual file, not a copy from the spool file.
-C	Copies to a spooling file before sending on to the destination machine.
-d	Creates a directory to match the directory sent from the source machine. (This is the default.)
-f	Does not create a directory to match the directory sent from the source machine.
-g*p*	Sets job priority to *p*.
-j	Prints job number.
-m	Notifies sender via mail when transfer is complete.

Continued

-n *user*	Notifies *user* via mail when transfer is complete.
-r	Queues the *file(s)*, but doesn't send them.
-s*file*	Send the transfer status to *file* (instead of to user, as specified by **-m**).
-x*n*	Debugs at level *n*; lowest is 1, highest is 9.

RELATED COMMANDS

ftp	File-transfer protocol.
mailx	Sends and receives mail.
rlogin	Remote login.
uulog	Logs **uucp** traffic.
uustat	Returns status of **uucp**.
uux	Executes command on remote system.

Communication
Commands

uudecode   Decode Encoded File

uudecode *file*

PURPOSE

Reads a file converted by **uuencode** and restores it to original form.

RELATED COMMAND

uuencode   Encodes file for **mailx**.

uuencode — Encode Binary File

unencode *file name* | **mailx** *username*

PURPOSE

Converts a binary *file* to an encoded form that can be sent with the **mailx** command. This encoded file is in ASCII form.

RELATED COMMANDS

mailx   Sends mail.

uudecode   Decodes file encoded by **uuencode**.

uulog · UNIX-to-UNIX Log

uulog *options*

PURPOSE

Keeps a log of **uucp** file transfers to and from a specified system.

OPTIONS

-f*system*   Applies the **-tail** command to display the
                   most recent file transfers.

-s*system*   Displays all actions on the specified *system*.

RELATED COMMAND

uucp   UNIX-to-UNIX copy.

uuname *options*

PURPOSE

Lists the UNIX system that can be accessed with UNIX communications tools like **mailx** or **uucp**.

Do not confuse *uuname* **with** *uname*.

N O T E

OPTIONS

-**c**   Prints system names that can be accessed with the **cu** command.

-**l**   Prints the name of the local system.

RELATED COMMANDS

cu   Calls up another system.

mailx Sends and receives mail.

uucp UNIX-to-UNIX copy.

uustat   UNIX-to-UNIX Status

uustat *options*

PURPOSE

Returns information about the current status of **uucp** commands. It can also be used to cancel **uucp** requests. Not all of these options are available on all systems.

OPTIONS

-a	Reports on the status for all jobs.
-c	Reports the average time spent in queue.
-d*n*	Reports average for the last *n* minutes (default is last hour).
-j	Reports the total number of jobs.
-k*id*	Kills job *id*; you must own the job.
-m	Shows what systems can be accessed.
-n	Shows standard output but not standard error.
-p	Runs **ps -flp** on current processes.
-q	Reports on the jobs queued for all systems.
-r*n*	Runs **touch** on its job *n*.
-s*system*	Reports the status of jobs on *system*.
-S*type*	Reports the status jobs of *type*:

c	Completed.
i	Interrupted.
q	Queued.
r	Running.

| **-t***system* | Reports the average transfer rate on *system*. |
| **-u***user* | Reports on the jobs started with *user*. |

RELATED COMMANDS

cu	Calls up another system.
mailx	Sends and receives mail.
uucp	UNIX-to-UNIX copy.

Communication
Commands

uux *options system! command*

PURPOSE

Runs a UNIX command on a remote UNIX system. It also copies files to and from other UNIX systems. A listing of permissible commands can be often be found on a remote system in **etc/uucp/permissions**.

OPTIONS

-a*user*	Notifies *user* when command is completed.
-b	Returns the input if an error interrupts the *command*.
-c	Copies the actual file, not a copy from the spool file.
-C	Copies to a spooling file before sending on to the destination machine.
-g*p*	Sets job priority to *p*.
-j	Prints **uux** job number.
-n	Does not send mail if the *command* fails.
-p	Uses standard input for *command*.
-r	Queues the *file(s)*, but doesn't send them.
-s*file*	Send the transfer status to *file*.
-x*n*	Debugs at level *n*; lowest is 1, highest is 9.
-z	Notifies user who initiated command when it is completed.

RELATED COMMANDS

mailx   Sends and receives mail.

rlogin   Remote login.

uucp   UNIX-to-UNIX copy.

vacation *options*

PURPOSE

Returns a mail message to the originator, indicating that you're on vacation. This lets people know you are not ignoring them. **vacation** is not available on all systems, and versions vary among systems.

OPTIONS

-F *user*
Forwards mail to user when *mailfile* is unavailable.

-l *logfile*
Logs names of senders in *logfile* (default is **$HOME/.maillog**).

-m *mailfile*
Saves messages in *mailfile* (default is **$HOME/.mailfile**).

-M *file*
Use *file* as the message sent to mail originators (default is **/usr/lib/mail/std_vac_msg**).

wall

PURPOSE

Sends a message to all users. After sending the message, end input with **Ctrl-D**. This command is most often used by system administrators to warn users about a pending system shutdown.

EXAMPLE

```
$ wall
WARNING: System will be shut down in 5 minutes.
```

(This sends a warning message to all users logged on the system.)

write   Write to User

write *user tty*

PURPOSE

Sends a text message to another user. Press **Ctrl-D** to exit.

EXAMPLE

```
$ write eric
Hi Eric
Ctrl-D
```

(This sends the message "Hi Eric" to user **eric**.)

6

System-Administration Commands

The system-administration commands are geared primarily toward the system administrator, and some of them are available only for privileged users. However, others—particularly the **at** command and other related commands—can also come in quite handy for the majority of UNIX system users. If you think that you could use any of these commands but are currently barred from doing so, check with your system administrator.

at *option1 time [date] increment*
at *option2 [job-id]*

PURPOSE

Performs specified commands at given times and dates, as long as the commands require no additional input from you. For instance, you may want to print a series of long documents at midnight, so that you won't tie up the laser printer for hours when other people may need it. You don't need to interact with the laser printer at midnight (although you should make sure its paper tray is filled before leaving work!); nevertheless, you can use the **at** command to print at midnight.

There are two sets of options are available with the **at** commands. One set of options, which we'll call *option1*, relates to setting the targeted time and date. The second set of options, which we'll represent with *option2*, allows changes to jobs already scheduled. After you enter the **at** command, you type in the commands to execute at that time. You type in these commands at the keyboard. When you're finished, press **Ctrl-D**. At the given time, **at** runs your commands. Any output from the commands is sent to you via electronic mail.

NOTE

Even though the *at* command is used primarily by system administrators, it can also be used by regular users, but this usage must be set by the system administrator. If you are not authorized to use *at*, you'll see an error message like the following: *at: you are not authorized to run at. Sorry.* If you want use of the *at* command, talk with your system administrator.

Continued

EXAMPLES

```
$ at 11am
ls
Ctrl-D
```

(**at** reads the command to run from standard input. On the
line following the command line, you enter commands and
then press **Ctrl-D**.)

```
$ at 11am nov 1
$ at 11am nov 1, 1994
$ at 11am sun
$ at now + 2 weeks
$ at [option2] [job-id]
```

> **Job-IDs are issued by the system when a job is
> scheduled.**

N O T E

SCHEDULING OPTIONS

-f filename   Executes the commands listed in *filename*.
Not available on all systems.

-m   Notifies user when job is completed.

TIME OPTIONS

time   Obviously, the time when the commands
should run. Unless you specify otherwise
(with am or pm as a suffix), the system
assumes military time.

Continued

midnight ⎫	These options are used in lieu of a specific
noon ⎬	time. If you use **now** as an option, you must
now ⎭	specify an increment (see below).

DATE OPTIONS

date　　　Format is usually specified as *month*, *day*, *year*, with *year* optional.

day　　　The specific day when the command should run, with the name either spelled out (*Sunday*) or referred to by the first three letters (*Sun*).

today ⎫	These options are used in lieu of a specific
tomorrow ⎭	date.

ALREADY-SCHEDULED JOBS OPTIONS

-l　　　Lists current job.

-r　　　Removes specified job.

INCREMENT OPTION

increment　　A numerical value relative to the current time and date. The *increment* must contain a reference to **minute**, **hour**, **day**, **week**, **month**, or **year**. In the example at the beginning of this command's listing (*at now + 2 weeks*), the job would be performed 2 weeks from now.

RELATED COMMANDS

atq	Immediately prints jobs scheduled with the **at** command.
atrm	Removes jobs scheduled by **at**.
batch	Runs a series of commands in order in the background.

atq *option user*

PURPOSE

Prints jobs already scheduled with the **at** command. There's not a lot of control with the command: You can print all the jobs, print all the jobs generated by a specific *user*, or print the jobs in the order they were generated through the **at** command.

 Even though the *atq* command is used primarily by system administrators, it can also be used by regular users, but this usage must be set by the system administrator. If you want use of the *atq* command, talk with your system administrator.

OPTIONS

-c   Sorts the print queue in the order jobs were generated through the **at** command.

-n   Returns the number of jobs in the print queue but does not print them.

RELATED COMMANDS

at   Schedules jobs to be performed at a specific time.

atrm   Removes jobs scheduled by **at**.

atrm *option user job-id*

PURPOSE

Removes jobs already scheduled with the **at** command. Privileged users can remove *all* jobs or the jobs of a specific user, while other users can remove only those jobs generated by themselves.

OPTIONS

-a   Removes all jobs generated only by the current user.

-i   Removes the job only after the approval of the user (**y** or **n**).

RELATED COMMANDS

at   Schedules jobs to be performed at a specific time.

atq   Immediately prints jobs scheduled with the **at** command.

System-Administration Commands

batch

PURPOSE

Runs a series of commands one command at a time in the background, avoiding the performance issue of running several commands simultaneously in the background.

EXAMPLE

```
batch
pr -a kevinstuff
lp kevinstuff
Ctrl-D
```

OPTIONS

None.

chgrp   Change Group

chgrp *options groupname filename(s)*

PURPOSE

Changes the ownership of a file or files to a new or existing group, specified by either name (stored in **/etc/group**) or ID number. File owners can use the command to change the ownership of only their own files, while privileged users can use this command to change ownership of any file. This command can also be used to change the IDs for an entire directory and the files within.

EXAMPLES

```
$ chgrp restricted kevin.report
```

(This changes the group for **kevin.report** to **restricted**.)

```
$ chgrp -R restricted /usr/users/kevin/reports
```

(This changes the group for all the files and subdirectories within **/usr/users/kevin/reports** to **restricted**.)

OPTIONS

-h   Changes a symbolic link, not the file referenced by a symbolic link. Not available on all systems.

-R   Recursively changes through subdirectories and files.

group   Either a groupname (stored in **/etc/group**) or ID number.

Continued

RELATED COMMANDS

chown	Changes file ownership.
chmod	Changes file-access permissions.
newgrp	Changes to a new working group.

cpio — Create Archive

cpio *options*

PURPOSE

Copies archived files to and from backup storage devices like tape drives. This rather involved command is meant for true system administrators, not for those of us who putz around with system-administration commands as the need arises. Because of this, we suggest that you check your system documentation before using this command. Besides, the **tar** command is much easier to work with.

crontab *filename*

PURPOSE

Sets up a file containing a list of tasks to be performed regularly, such as data backups and regular correspondence. The **crontab** command creates the file from keyboard entry (if none exists) or processes a text file generated by a text editor. The **cron** program then runs those commands.

 The syntax of this file is very rigid. There are six fields to a file, each separated by a space. The first five fields specify exactly when the command is to be run; the sixth field is the command itself. The five fields are:

Field	Meaning
1	Minutes after the hour (0–59)
2	Hour, in 24-hour format (0–23)
3	Day of the month (1–31)
4	Month (1–12)
5	Day of the week (0–6; the 0 refers to Sunday)

Asterisks (*) specify when commands are to be run in every instance of the value of the field. For instance, an asterisk in the Month field would mean that the command should be run every month. In addition, multiple events can be scheduled within a field; merely separate all instances with commas—with no space between.

EXAMPLES

To run a command every morning at 9:30 a.m., the line in the **crontab**-generated file would look like this:

```
30 9 * * * command
```

To run a command at 1 p.m. only on the 1st and 15th of the month, the line in the **crontab**-generated file would look like this:

```
0 13 1,15 * * command
```

To install the events file in your system, making it operational, use the **crontab** command:

```
$ crontab events_file
```

NOTE Although *crontab* is a command primarily meant for system administrators, it's helpful for any user. BSD or pre-System V users, however, are out of luck, as those systems allow use of *crontab* only for system administrators. If you're using a newer version of UNIX and want to use this command, check with your system administrator.

OPTIONS

-e   Edits the current **crontab** file or creates a new one. Not available on all systems.

-l   Lists the contents of the **crontab** file.

-r   Removes the **crontab** file.

RELATED COMMAND

at   Runs a command at a specified time.

login   Login System

login *options*

PURPOSE

Logs you on the UNIX system. Without this command, there's not a lot of computing work you can finish. If you do not supply a username with the **login** command, you'll be prompted for one. In addition, **login** may ask you for a password, if your system is so configured.

OPTIONS

username   Supply a *username* when you login.

var=value   Changes the *value* of an environment variable.

RELATED COMMAND

logname   Login name.

newgrp   New Group

newgrp *option group*

PURPOSE

Logs you into a new *group* during a current session. If
you do not have permission to join a group, the request
will be denied.

OPTION

-              Changes to the new group, with new envi-
               ronment associated with the new *group*.

RELATED COMMANDS

chgrp   Changes group.
env   Sets environment.

stty *options modes*

PURPOSE

Displays your terminal configuration and options. If you use **stty** with no options or modes, your current configuration will be returned in basic format; use **stty -a** for a more complete—and cryptic—listing of your current configuration.

    As UNIX hardware evolves, the use of the **stty** command becomes less and less common. Unless you're really into hardware and want to start mucking around with modes and settings, we advise you to shy away from the **stty** command, except in one situation: When you dial into a UNIX host and find that the **Backspace** key does not work. Try the following:

```
$ stty erase backspace
```

Don't type the word *backspace*; instead, press the actual **Backspace** key on your terminal. This should fix the problem.

OPTIONS

-a   Displays current options and their settings.

-g   Displays current settings.

tput   Query Terminal

tput *options capname*

PURPOSE

Displays information about your terminal's capabilities, as contained in the **terminfo** database (usually stored in the **/usr/lib/terminfo** directory). While you can use the **tput** command to manipulate your terminal directly—for instance, the command **tput clear** will clear the screen—this capability is used mostly by programmers and certainly not beginning UNIX users.

OPTIONS

-T*type*   Returns the capabilities of terminal *type*. If no *type* is specified, **tput** uses the current terminal as the default.

init   Returns initialization strings and expands tabs.

longname   Returns the long name of your terminal.

System-Administration Commands

RELATED COMMAND

stty   Sets terminal modes.

tty *options*

PURPOSE

Returns the operational settings for your terminal. This command is often used in shell scripts to see if the script is being run from a terminal.

OPTIONS

-a   Displays all settings; not available on all systems.

-s   Displays only codes: 0 (terminal), 1 (not a terminal), or 2 (invalid option).

RELATED COMMANDS

stty   Change terminal settings.

7

Shell Commands and Variables

A **shell** is a command like every other UNIX command. If you've already browsed through the commands listed in Section 5, "UNIX Commands, Organized by Groups," you'll see that the C shell, the Bourne shell, and the Korn shell were all listed as commands. All three shells do the same thing: They act as interpreters, translating your commands into a form the operating system can understand. When you log in a UNIX system, you automatically launch a shell program; without it, you wouldn't be able to do a whole lot with UNIX.

As noted in Section 1, "UNIX Overview: Commands and Structures," a shell uses a special symbol to show that it's ready and waiting for a command from you. The Bourne and Korn shells typically use the $ symbol, while the C shell uses the % symbol. (If you're logged on the system as a privileged user—also known as the superuser or the root user—you'll have a # as your prompt.)

Most users configure their system with the shell when they log in the system (this is known as setting your *environment variables*, contained in a file referenced in your **.profile** file) or perform some special tasks with **shell scripts**. The analog to DOS batch files, shell scripts are exactly what the name implies: They are a script of commands performed by the system on command.

This section covers the most importat shell variables followed by some choice shell commands. We do not cover *every* shell variable, nor do we cover *every* shell command. Using variables and shell commands is considered an intermediate to advanced topic; see the Bibliography for a listing of books that will help you on your way in advanced shell usage.

Bourne and Korn Shells Variables

The Bourne shell has the distinction of being the original shell in UNIX. The newer Korn shell was designed as an improvement over the Bourne shell, incorporating several useful traits from the C shell (such as command history) while retaining the familiar structure of the Bourne shell. Unless noted, the variables listed below are valid for both the Korn and Bourne shells. This is not a full list of shell variables, but merely the most useful and popular ones. Check your documentation or a book listed in the Bibliography for more information on shell variables.

Variable	Meaning
CDPATH	Tells the shell where to look for a relative pathname, which allows you to enter shorter command lines. For instance, if you used the following line:
	CDPATH=/usr/users/kevin/data
	in your **.profile** file, you wouldn't need to refer to the full pathname every time you wanted to refer to that directory. You can list multiple directories, so long as they are separated by colons (:).
COLUMNS	Sets the number of columns across your display. The default is 80. (Korn shell.)
EDITOR	Sets the default text editor, usually **emacs** or **vi**. Some commands and other applications call an editor. (Korn shell.)
ENV	Establishes the location of the environment file (usually **.kshrc**). (Korn shell.)
HISTSIZE	Sets the history list size. *History* refers to commands already executed; the list can be referenced on the command line by number. (Korn shell.)

Variable	Meaning
HOME	When you login a system, you're immediately placed in your **HOME** directory. When you use the **cd** command with no parameters, you're automatically placed back into that directory.
IFS	Stands for *I*nternal *F*ield *S*eparator. The prompt uses spaces, tabs, and newlines to separate items on a command line. If you were to set the **IFS** to **&**, the prompt would use that symbol to separate items on a command line.
LOGNAME	Stores the name of the current user's login name. (Korn shell.)
MAIL	Designates your mail file, where **mailx** or another mail program automatically sends your incoming mail.
MAILCHECK	Tells the shell how often to check for mail (the default is every 10 minutes), measured in seconds. A setting of **MAILCHECK=3600** checks for mail every hour; a setting of **MAILCHECK=0** checks for mail every time a prompt appears on the screen (which is not the most efficient use of computing resources).
MAILPATH	Designates multiple mail files.
PATH	Sets the file-search path. If you screw up and mistakenly have the system check for multiple files, you could end up spending a lot of time as the shell searches through a large file system. Since most of your frequently used files are in the same directories, this allows you to tell the system where to look for commands.

Variable	Meaning
PS1	Stands for Primary Shell prompt (the default is $). A line like **PS1="Wake up!"** would establish a prompt of **Wake up!**
PS2	Sets the secondary shell prompt (the default is >). The secondary prompt is used when a command runs over a single line.
SHELL	Sets the subshell, which is used by commands like **vi** or **ed**.
TERM	Stands for *term*inal type. For instance, a setting of **TERM=VT100** sets the terminal type for VT100, which is a popular terminal type.
TERMINFO	Stands for *term*inal *info*rmation, stored in the **/usr/lib/terminfo** database. (Korn shell.)
TMOUT	Sets the timeout value, the period of inactivity (in seconds) before the system logs a user out. (Korn shell.)
TZ	Stands for *t*ime *z*one, which is referenced by the **date** command. For instance, if you were in the Central Time Zone with daylight savings time, you'd normally use **TZ=CST6CDT**. (Korn shell.)

The time zone format may be different on your version of UNIX. Check your system documentation.

NOTE

271

C Shell Variables

The C shell dates from the 1970s, when it was originated at the University of California as a more advanced shell. This shell is so named because of its resemblance to the C programming language, although it does make for a nice little pun.

The following list does not contain all the shell variables, but merely the most useful and popular ones. Check your documentation or a book listed in the Bibliography for more information on shell variables.

Variable	Meaning
cdpath	Tells the shell where to look for a relative pathname, which allows you to enter shorter command lines. For instance, if you used the following line: **cdpath=/usr/users/kevin/data** in your **.cshrc** file, you wouldn't need to refer to the full pathname every time you wanted to refer to that directory. You can list multiple directories, so long as they are separated by colons (:).
echo	Displays full commands, including substitutions.
history	Sets the history list size. *History* refers to commands already executed; the list can be referenced on the command line by number. (Korn shell.)
HOME	When you log in a system, you're immediately placed in your **HOME** directory. When you use the **cd** command, you're automatically placed back into that directory.

Variable	Meaning
mail	Designates your mail file, where **mailx** or another mail program automatically sends your incoming mail.
notify	Informs you when a job is completed.
PATH	Sets the file-search path. If you screw up and mistakenly have the system check for multiple files, you could end up spending a lot of time as the shell searches through a large file system. Since most of your frequently used files are in the same directories, this allows you to tell the system where to look for commands.
prompt	Sets the prompt, which informs you that the shell is waiting for a command. The default is %.
savehist	Determines the number of commands to be saved in your **.history** file, which received input thanks to the **history** command.
shell	Sets the subshell, which is used by commands like **vi** or **ed**.
TERM	Stands for *term*inal type. For instance, a setting of **TERM=VT100** sets the terminal type for VT100, which is a popular terminal type.
USER	Stores the name of the current user's login name.

Shell Commands and Scripts

When you use a shell, you enter commands at the shell's prompt (usually $ or %). You can enter any of the commands described in this book in Sections 5 and 6, as well as a number of shell commands. These commands exist only in a particular shell, such as the **alias** command in the C shell (described under "C Shell Commands", below).

In addition to entering commands at the prompt, you can also write **shell scripts**, which are sets of shell commands stored in an ASCII text file. Shell scripts are an easy way to store commonly used sets of UNIX commands. (DOS users call shell scripts **batch files**.) In DOS, these files have a **.BAT** extension. In UNIX, though, you are free to name your shell scripts anything you desire (providing you desire a valid UNIX filename, of course).

Shell scripts use both the same commands that you could type in at the shell prompt ($ or %) and some of the complex commands described below. It's usually easier to write a shell script and use it as needed than to reissue the commands whenever you want to do a common task.

You'll find that many of the following commands smack of programming. No, we're not out to make you programmers. But it is useful to know what these commands do, especially if you need to write a short shell script on your own. For more advanced shell scripting, check your documentation or a book listed in the Bibliography.

Empowering a Shell Script to Run

You store shell scripts in ASCII text files. Before you can try out a shell script, you must tell UNIX that your ASCII text file really does contain commands. To do this, you can use the **chmod** command (described in Section 5, "UNIX Commands, Organized by Group"):

```
$ chmod +x my_shell_script
```

You need to enable the execute permission on the shell script's file. In the above example, we used **chmod** to enable the execute permission (**+x**) on the file **my_shell_script**.

Once you do this, you can execute your shell script by typing in the filename. For example:

```
$ my_shell_script
```

Comments

It's always wise to describe what a shell script does, so that when you look it up months from now you know why you originally wrote it. To help describe what is going on, you can include **comments**. A comment in a shell script starts with a # character at the start of the line. Any other text—to the end of the line—is treated as a comment; that is, the shell ignores this text. For example:

```
# This is a comment.
```

Comments apply equally to the Bourne, Korn, and C shells.

Bourne and Korn Shell Commands

When you're writing shell scripts, you often need to control what happens based on certain conditions. For example, you may want to copy the 1994 report to another directory using the **cp** command. But, if the 1994 report is not done yet (that is, if the file does not exist), you may want to take other action, such as notifying the user that the report is missing. You can use the **echo** command to display a message for the user. But you don't want to run both the **echo** command (with an error message) and the **cp** command. To control which command gets executed, you can use the **if-then** command.

If-Then

The Bourne and Korn shells allow you to run a command (or set of many commands) only under certain conditions. The problem is that you must format these conditions in a way that the shell understands. Format your **if-then** commands in the following way:

> **if test** *expression*
>   **then**
>   *command1*
>   *command2*
>   *command3*
>   ...
>   **fi**

Basically, **if-then** uses the built-in **test** command (which we cover below) to determine whether or not to run a set of commands. These commands are placed after **then** and before **fi**. (Fi stands for if backward.) You can place any number of commands you need between **then** and **fi**. For example:

```
# Check if 5 is indeed 5.
if test 5 = 5
   then
        echo "5 equals 5"
fi
```

This example tests whether 5 is the same as 5. If so, it echoes (prints out) a statement to that effect.

The Test Command

The **test** command is both a UNIX command and a shell command. **Test** returns a true value if the expression you pass to it is true. Otherwise, **test** returns a false value. The shell **if** command then uses **test** to determine whether or not to execute the code between **then** and **fi**.

You can use many options with **test** when writing complex shell scripts. Most of these options delve into areas far too advanced for this beginning book. One option that you'll see a lot in shell script files, though, is the cryptic use of square brackets. You can use square bracket [ ] as a shorthand for the **test** command. For example:

```
if [ 5 = 5 ]
    then
        echo "5 still equals 5"
fi
```

For other **test** options, check your documentation or a book listed in the Bibliography.

If-Then-Else

Sometimes you need to perform a set of commands if the condition in an **if-then** command is *not* met, as well as if the condition is met. In that case, you can use **if-then-else**, which uses the following format:

> **if test** *expression*
> **then**
>   *command1*
>   *command2*
>   *command3*
>   ...
> **else**
>   *command1*
>   *command2*
>   *command3*
>   ...
>   **fi**

If the **test** expression is true, then the shell executes the commands between **then** and **else**. Otherwise, the shell executes the commands between **else** and **fi**.

For example:

```
if test 4 = 5
    then
        echo "4 equals 5"
    else
        echo "4 does not equal 5"
fi
```

If you run this, you should see that four does not equal five.

For Loops

The **for** command allows you to write a shell script that loops through a set of values, performing the same commands repeatedly. Most commonly, you want to loop through a set of files and perform the same operation on each file. The **for** command repeats a set of commands over a set of values for a given variable. The **for** command uses the following format:

> **for** *variable*
> **in** *values*
> **do**
>   *command1*
>   *command2*
>   *command3*
>   ...
> **done**

It often is important to place the **in** statement on its own line.

All commands between **do** and **done** get executed each time through the loop. Each time through the loop, your *variable* will have one of the values. For example:

```
for filename
    in *.1994
    do
```

```
    echo $filename
done
```

The variable **filename** will hold the name of a file ending in *.1994*, such as **jan.1994**, **feb.1994**, and **dec.1994**, each time through the loop.

C Shell Commands

The C shell provides the same basic set of control commands, such as **if-then-else**, as do the Bourne and Korn shells. But the C shell uses its own syntax, which tends to be confusing at times.

If-Then

Like the Bourne and Korn shells, the C shell provides an **if-then** statement. In the C shell, it has a slightly different format:

> **if** *(expression)* **then**
>   *command1*
>   *command2*
>   *command3*
>
>   ...
> **endif**

For example:

```
if (5 == 5) the,
    echo "5 does indeed equal 5"
endif
```

Note the use of == (two equal signs) rather than =. In addition, with the C shell, you must place **then** on the same line as **if**.

If-Then-Else

You can also use an **if-then-else** statement:

> **if** *(expression)* **then**
> > *command1*
> > *command2*
> > *command3*
> > ...
>
> **else**
> > *command1*
> > *command2*
> > *command3*
> > ...
>
> **endif**

For example:

```
if (4 == 5) then
    echo "4 equals 5"
  else
    echo "4 does not equal 5"
endif
```

This example should print out:

```
4 does not equal 5
```

Foreach

Instead of a command named **for**, the C shell provides a **foreach** command, but the effect is nearly the same:

> **foreach** *variable (list-of-values)*
> > *command1*
> > *command2*
> > *command3*
> > ...
>
> **end**

For example:

```
foreach filename (*.1994)
      echo $filename
end
```

This example lists all files that end with *.1994*. Each time through the loop, the variable **filename** holds one of the filenames (ending in *.1994*).

Using Alias to Change Identities

In addition to the commands above, the C shell offers the handy **alias** command:

alias *new-name old-command*

For example, if you're more experienced with DOS than UNIX, you may be confused by all the options to the UNIX **ls** command. With **alias**, you can define your own command named *dir*, which acts more closely to the DOS **DIR** command:

```
alias dir      ls -alx
```

This command aliases **dir** for the more complex (and harder to remember) command of **ls -alx**. Thus, when you type in **dir**, the C shell actually executes **ls -alx**, so you'll see a long-format directory listing, which is about the closest UNIX equivalent to the DOS **DIR** command. With **alias**, you're extending the set of commands offered by UNIX. This is very useful, particularly if you're moving to UNIX from another operating system, like DOS or VMS.

Shell
Commands

8

FTP Commands

One undeniable advantage of being on the Internet is widely available free software. While we often dial into remote machines and grab interesting software, this process is not easy for the average computer user. As with almost everything else in the UNIX world, the commands are geared for the expert—in other words, someone who already knows what they are doing.

If you are on the Internet, you can use the **ftp** program to transfer files to and from remote machines. (If you're not sure about being on the Internet, check with your system administrator.) **Ftp** stands for *F*ile *T*ransfer *P*rotocol, and it's rapidly becoming the most popular way to grab files from another networked computer. The **ftp** program is easy to use. To start it, type

```
$ ftp
ftp>
```

Your shell prompt will be replaced with an **ftp** prompt. At this point you would enter the commands listed in this section.

You can establish a direct connection to a machine either by specifying the machine's name when you begin an **ftp** session:

Ftp
Commands

```
$ ftp machine_kevin
```

or by using the **open** command after starting an **ftp**
session:

```
ftp> open
(to) machine_kevin
Connected to machine_kevin
```

Anonymous ftp

Normally, when you use the **ftp** command, you must
have an account set up on the remote machine. Since it's
rather impractical to set up an account for every user in
a high-traffic situation, the practice of **anonymous ftp**
evolved. This allows you to log on a remote machine as
anonymous. Your privileges on the machine are
extremely limited—you're allowed mainly to upload and
download files from a specific directory, and that's
about it—but this setup works very well.

To use anonymous ftp, you initiate an **ftp** session in
the normal way. The difference is that you enter *anonymous* as your name, with your electronic-mail address
(referred to as your *ident*) as your password:

```
ftp> open
(to) machine_kevin
Connected to machine_kevin
Name (machine_kevin): anonymous
220 Guest login ok, send ident as password.
Password: kreichard@mcimail.com
230 Guest login ok, access restrictions apply.
```

From there you use the regular **ftp** commands.

A Listing of ftp Commands

Here's a rundown on the commands to use once you're online. If you're not sure about what command to use, don't be afraid to experiment. You can't do a whole lot of damage, and the worse that can happen is you might be booted off the system.

 Some of the commands used during an *ftp* session are standard UNIX commands. We've flagged them for you, should you want more information.

Command	Purpose
! *command*	Runs a shell.
$ *macros arg(s)*	Runs a *macro*, along with an optional *arg*ument.
? *command*	Displays help for specified *command*.
account *password*	Sets up a new account, with a new *password*.
append *file1 file2*	Appends the local file *file1* to the remote file *file2*.
ascii	Sets transfer mode to ASCII (text) format. This is the default.
bell	Creates a sound (usually a beep) after a file is transferred.
binary	Sets transfer mode to binary format.
bye	Ends ftp session and ends the **ftp** program.
cd *directory*	Changes the current remote directory to *directory*. THIS IS A STANDARD UNIX COMMAND. SEE SECTION 4, "UNIX FROM A TO Z", TO SEARCH FOR MORE INFORMATION ON THIS COMMAND.

Command	Purpose
cdup	Changes the current directory to one level up on the directory hierarchy. Same as **cd**.
close	Ends ftp session with the remote machine but continues the **ftp** command on the local machine.
delete *filename*	Removes *filename* from remote directory.
debug	Turns debugging on or off. (The default is off.)
dir *directory filename*	Returns the contents of the specified *directory*; resulting information is stored in *filename* as specified.
disconnect	Ends ftp session and **ftp** program.
get *file1 file2*	Gets *file1* from the remote machine and stores it under the filename *file2*. If *file2* is not specified, the *file1* name will be retained. THIS COMMAND WORKS THE SAME AS THE **RECV** COMMAND.
hash	Returns status while transferring numbers by returning feedback for each block transferred.
help *command*	Displays information about specified *command*; displays general help information if no *command* is specified.
lcd *directory*	Changes the current local directory to the specified *directory*. If *directory* is not specified, the current local directory changes to the home directory.

Command	Purpose
ls *directory filename*	Lists the contents of the directory (if *directory* is specified; otherwise, the contents of the current directory will be listed). If a *filename* is specified, then information about the specified file will be listed. THIS COMMAND IS A STANDARD UNIX COMMAND. SEE SECTION 4, "UNIX FROM A TO Z", FOR MORE INFORMATION ON THIS COMMAND.
macdef *macrofile*	Defines a macro, ending with a blank line; the resulting macro is stored in the file *macrofile*.
mdelete *filename(s)*	Deletes *filename(s)* on the remote machine.
mdir *filename(s)*	Returns directory for multiple, specified *filename(s)*.
mget *filename(s)*	Gets the specified multiple *filename(s)* from the remote machine.
mkdir *directory*	Makes a new directory, named *directory*, on the remote machine. **MKDIR** IS A STANDARD UNIX COMMAND. SEE SECTION 4, "UNIX FROM A TO Z", FOR MORE INFORMATION ON THIS COMMAND.
mput *filename(s)*	Puts the specified *filename(s)* on the remote machine.
open *remote_machine*	Opens a connection to the specified remote machine. If no remote machine is specified, the system will prompt you for a machine name.

Command	Purpose
put *file1 file2*	Puts local file *file1* on the remote machine, under the new filename *file2*. If *file2* is not specified, the file will remain with the name *file1*. THIS COMMAND WORKS THE SAME AS THE **SEND** COMMAND.
pwd	Returns the current directory on the remote machine. (No, this command has nothing to do with a password. This acronym actually stands for *p*rint *w*orking *d*irectory, if you find this easier to remember.) **PWD** IS A STANDARD UNIX COMMAND. SEE SECTION 4, "UNIX FROM A TO Z", FOR MORE INFORMATION ON THIS COMMAND.
rmdir *directory*	Removes *directory* from the remote machine. **RMDIR** IS A STANDARD UNIX COMMAND. SEE SECTION 4, "UNIX FROM A TO Z", FOR MORE INFORMATION ON THIS COMMAND.
quit	Terminates connection to remote machine and ends the **ftp** program.
recv *file1 file2*	Retrieves *file1* from remote machine and stores it as *file2* on your computer (if you specify *file2*, that is). THIS COMMAND WORKS THE SAME AS THE **GET** COMMAND.
remotehelp *command*	Returns help information about a specific *command* from the remote machine, not from the help files on your computer.

Command	Purpose
rename *file1 file2*	Renames *file1* on the remote system to the new *file2*.
rmdir *directory*	Removes *directory* from the remote machine. **RMDIR** IS A STANDARD UNIX COMMAND. SEE SECTION 4, "UNIX FROM A TO Z," FOR MORE INFORMATION ON THIS COMMAND.
send *file1 file2*	Puts local file *file1* on the remote machine, under the new filename *file2*. If *file2* is not specified, the file will be remain with the name *file1*. THIS COMMAND WORKS THE SAME AS THE **PUT** COMMAND.

Related Commands

Command	Purpose
rcp	Remote copy; found in Section 5, "UNIX Commands, Organized by Groups" as a Communication Command.
rlogin	Remote login; found in Section 5, "UNIX Commands, Organized by Groups" as a Communication Command.

Bibliography

If you've selected this book from the shelves of your friendly community bookstore, you've already discovered that there are a lot of UNIX books on the market. Most of them are on the advanced level and are geared toward programmers and system administrators. Other titles are geared for a small, specialized audience (most UNIX users won't need guides on **sendmail** and **perl**, for instance). If you focus only on the titles meant for the larger end-user community, you have a much smaller list of UNIX books. From these books we've put together the following list of recommended books.

Tutorials

Teach Yourself UNIX. Kevin Reichard and Eric F. Johnson, MIS:Press, 1992. This intro to the UNIX operating system was designed as a companion to this book. Most of the commands listed in this work are more fully explained in *Teach Yourself UNIX*, while the underlying concepts of UNIX are explained in depth.

Learning the UNIX Operation System. Grace Todino, John Strange, and Jerry Peek, O'Reilly & Associates, 1993. A terse introduction to some basic UNIX concepts.

General Titles

UNIX System V Release 4: An Introduction for New and Experienced Users. Kenneth Rosen, Richard Rosinski, and James Farber, Osborne McGraw-Hill, 1990. This 1,200-page guide to UNIX is the most thorough documentation of SVR4 in one volume.

Life With UNIX: A Guide for Everyone. Don Libes and Sandy Ressler, Prentice Hall, 1989. A witty guide to UNIX, more interesting for its account of UNIX's development over the years.

UNIX in a Nutshell. Daniel Gilly, O'Reilly & Associates, 1992. More than you ever wanted to learn about UNIX commands.

Text Editing and Processing

Troff Typesetting for UNIX Systems. Sandra Emersom and Karen Paulsell, Prentice-Hall, 1987. More than one typesetter cut their teeth on troff and UNIX-based typesetting systems, as this guide shows.

The Ultimate Guide to the vi and ex Text Editors. Hewlett-Packard Co., Benjamin Cummings, 1990. Though largely superseded by graphical text editors, **vi** remains a very popular text editor in the UNIX world (though **ex** is for the most part obsolete). With the right guidance—such as shown in this work—**vi** can be a very useful tool.

Index

Commands are listed in bold type.